ISRAEL EATS

ISRAEL EATS

STEVEN ROTHFELD

with an Introduction by
NANCY SILVERTON

GIBBS SMITH
TO ENRICH AND INSPIRE HUMANKIND

Published by
Gibbs Smith
P.O. Box 667
Layton, Utah 84041

1.800.835.4993 orders
www.gibbs-smith.com

Designed by Rita Sowins / Sowins Design
Printed and bound in Hong Kong

Gibbs Smith books are printed on either recycled, 100% post-
consumer waste, FSC-certified papers or on paper produced
from sustainable PEFC-certified forest/controlled wood source.
Learn more at www.pefc.org.

Library of Congress Cataloging-in-Publication Data

Names: Rothfeld, Steven, author.
Title: Israel eats / Steven Rothfeld ;
with an introduction by Nancy Silverton.
Description: First edition. | Layton, Utah : Gibbs Smith, [2016] |
Includes index.
Identifiers: LCCN 2015033187 | ISBN 9781423640363
Subjects: LCSH: Cooking, Israeli. | Israel,—Pictorial works. |
LCGFT: Cookbooks.
Classification: LCC TX724 .R594 2016 | DDC 641.595694—dc23
LC record available at http://lccn.loc.gov/2015033187

To WAZE, the navigation app that made it possible for me to find my way to the gifted, generous, and courageous Israeli farmers, cooks, chefs, and artisans who opened both their doors and their hearts to me. With the frequent variations every few kilometers in the English spellings of the towns, and the Hebrew and Arabic scripts that I cannot read, I never would have been on time to my memorable meals nor would I have had the opportunity to converse with the many remarkable people who inspired this book. Thank you, Israeli WAZE creators: Amir Shinar, Ehud Shabtai, and Uri Levine.

HALF TITLE PAGE: LUNCH AT GOATS WITH THE WIND IN YODFAT. **TITLE PAGE:** ROASTED VEGETABLES AT CLARO IN TEL AVIV. **PREVIOUS OVERLEAF:** A BAKER PREPARING MANAKISH ON THE SAJ AT HAGOLAN BAKERY IN MAJDAL SHAMS. **THIS IMAGE:** A VIEW FROM THE BEGINNING OF THE MA'ALE AKRABBIM (SCORPION'S ASCENT) IN THE SOUTH. IT IS AN ANCIENT ROUTE THAT PREDATES BIBLICAL TIMES AND HAS ALWAYS BEEN USED TO CONNECT THE ARAVA VALLEY TO THE CENTRAL NEGEV. THE BIBLE INCLUDES THIS ASCENT AS ONE OF THE BORDERS OF THE PROMISED LAND.

INTRODUCTION

ON A SHINY, SLATE-COLORED November afternoon in 1984, I was on a train crossing northern Italy. I had just finished admiring the Pisanello princesses in Verona and was on my way to look at Giotto's frescoes in Padua. I was sitting in an empty compartment and the door slid open. A man about my own age entered and sat down. We spoke about what we had seen and where we were planning to go. He had an accent that I couldn't quite place, and apropos of nothing in particular—except maybe noticing an American Jew in his twenties, intent on experiencing the art and architecture steeped in the traditions of the Catholic Church—he bluntly asked, "So you're a Jew . . . Why don't you go to Israel?" I realized he was Israeli and I ransacked my mind for an answer. "I'm not ready," I said. He glared at me impatiently. "For what?" he inquired, almost accusingly. Fragments of the darkening sky and moody Italian landscape flashed through the window and across my eyes. "To leave this," I replied, turning my head to the view.

I was fascinated by everything European and couldn't propel myself beyond what I knew about the Jews who had lived there and their ultimate fate. It could have been me, I thought, when I studied the memorial plaques on the streets in France, lit a candle to place on the ovens at Terezin, or saw my family name etched on the marble slab of a Holocaust memorial in the center of Paris. I couldn't conjure up a modern Jewish state in my mind or fully understand why I had no desire to see Israel, yet this brief exchange on the Italian train haunted me for years.

A quarter century after that meeting, I read Amos Oz's memoir, *A Tale Of Love and Darkness*, and devoured A. B. Yehoshua's novels about quirky contemporary life in Israel. I started to imagine the Israeli streets and towns with people living in them. Then in 2010, I had two weeks between assignments in Italy and decided to visit my friend Dorit in Israel. We had met as students at Art Center College of Design in the early 1980s and, like her compatriot on the train, she never could understand why I had not visited Israel.

So I left Italy behind and traveled to Israel. In the short time I spent wandering around this small country notorious for sorrow and conflict, I discovered joy, humor, celebration, endless holidays, and a vibrant cuisine. I had been so focused on the suffering of the Jews that the idea of the Israelis pursuing pleasure and eating great food never entered my mind. In markets with freshly squeezed pomegranate juice flowing wherever I turned; with mountains of marbled halvah flavored with chocolate, cilantro, coffee, and pesto; with fresh dates from farms near the Dead Sea; with steamy, flat, round and twisted breads; with dazzling displays of freshly caught Mediterranean fish and teetering stacks of cauliflower orbs, I encountered a world I had never imagined existed in Israel.

People were experiencing the joy of eating well in small hummuserias, seaside restaurants, market stalls, and chic dining rooms in Tel Aviv and Jerusalem. I was reminded of something I had once overheard an Italian mother say to her small child who was shoving a forkful of pasta into his mouth: *Buona, eh? Che gioia di mangiare* (Good, isn't it? What a joy it is to eat).

What I discovered on my first journey to Israel ignited a desire to explore this small country further and taste what they were cooking up on top of the layers of civilization that are still smoking. A friend told me that people under pressure are more creative. Does that explain why there are so many good things to eat in Israel?

When I taste something surprisingly delicious anywhere in the world, I often think of the chef Nancy Silverton. We have worked together on three books, and I have always marveled at how she will sample a sauce or nibble a morsel of bread and gently steer the cook or baker in the right direction. Her intuition about flavor verges on the supernatural. It was only natural, then, that when I conceived of the idea to do this book, I asked her to help me with it. A few months after I returned from my first visit to Israel, I showed her images from my trip, shared the stories of what I had seen and tasted there, and asked her to be a part of the project.

Nancy was skeptical about being involved with a book about Israeli cuisine and food culture. Her first visit to Israel had been in 1967, just months after the Six-Day War. She said her parents almost got divorced because her father wanted her to go and her mother was terrified at the idea. In the end, she did go and remembers that she was not at all impressed by the food. Shortly after she arrived in Tel Aviv, Nancy wrote home, "The food here is really terrible. The first two days I didn't eat or drink anything and I almost fainted. The nurse had to give me smelling salts, so now I force myself to eat."

I remember saying to her that at thirteen years old in 1967, she likely only ate hamburgers and french fries. Nancy laughed and said that was true; the only food she remembers from that trip was from the hamburger chain Wimpy.

Still, her interest was piqued, and over the next four years I continually updated her on the travails of finding a publisher who was courageous enough to invest in a book about a place the world takes notice of only when disaster strikes.

NANCY In 2012, I was intrigued, not only by Steven's updates—complete with all his infectious, passionate enthusiasm—but by Yotam Ottolenghi and his book *Jerusalem*.

Yet I really didn't know what Israeli food was. Back in 1967, we had tasted street food—falafel and shawarma—and I had liked some of it, but I really had no idea what I had been eating. Now, forty-eight years later, I was anxious to try what people were telling me was this exciting "new cuisine" of Israel.

So I agreed to meet Steven in Jerusalem right after the Passover holidays. I had such a backward outlook on what Israel was about, not only the food but also the style, the hotels, and even the people. When I arrived at the Mamilla Hotel I was stunned. It was so beautiful that for a second I thought I was at the Hôtel de Paris in Monte Carlo. Our first night was the eve of Holocaust Memorial Day and most of the town's restaurants were closed, so we ate at the hotel. This was my first inkling that food was

---

PREVIOUS PAGE, TOP: ABULAFIA BAKERY IN JAFFA. PREVIOUS PAGE, BOTTOM: POMEGRANATES IN MAHANE YEHUDA MARKET, JERUSALEM. OVERLEAF: DALIAH SHPIGEL'S OPEN-AIR KITCHEN ON HER FARM GOATS WITH THE WIND IN YODFAT.

taken very seriously here. Unlike so many hotel dining rooms, this restaurant was surprisingly excellent. There was no menu and the chef sent us a seventy-two-hour organic chicken; grouper shawarma with a spicy tomato salad and smoked black tahini; and a sea bass fillet with caramelized turnip, kohlrabi, cabbage, black garlic and cashews in an herbal infused olive oil, and right then and there I knew that either I or Israeli food had come a long, long way since 1967.

The next day, chef Tomer Niv, from Rama's Kitchen in Netaf, took us on a tasting tour in the Old City market. We ate fresh pita, lamb kabobs, and Arab pastries. We tasted Middle Eastern spices and freshly ground raw yellow tahini, and it was here that I first had the hummus and falafel that made clear to me that the renditions in America are pale imitations.

When you talk about Israeli cooking, you might, like I did in my naïveté, think of Jewish cooking, or, more specifically, Jewish American cooking, which is nothing like what I was tasting. And you would be, as I was, simply wrong. The cuisine of Israel is an extraordinary layering of flavors. The flavors are complex but in harmony. The dishes are sometimes exotic but always approachable.

In contrast, for example, I have had exotic flavor combinations in various parts of the world that I have no interest in re-creating. Nor would I know how to do it. But in Israel, the combinations were sometimes complex, sometimes simple, yet always fresh and vibrant. Everything was marinated and seasoned so correctly that I was inspired. I talk about this in one of the headnotes of a recipe later in this book, but I have to say it here also: I love the use of torn and sometimes even whole herbs. They brighten every dish they touch.

I want to step away from the cuisine for a moment and talk about style. There's Roman chic and Parisian chic and Moscow chic. And many other places that are chic and stylish. But I was surprised, once again because of my naïveté, to find that some of the most stylish and chic places I have ever been to are in Israel. The kitchen of Erez Komarovsky, the museum and living quarters of Ilana Goor, and the kitchen at Goats with the Wind evoke style without looking styled.

People take vacations for various reasons. Some go for history, some for adventure, some for relaxation. I go for food. Before this trip, I would never have thought of Israel as a food destination. Now, I'll never think of Israel without thinking about the wonderful cuisine. In fact, the only controversy this trip has caused me is when I tell people—people who know I go to Italy every summer for six weeks—that across the board, the best food I've ever had on a vacation was on my recent trip to Israel. But that's controversy I embrace because it opens the door for me to tell them that in its food, in its style, in its hospitality, Israel was not at all what I expected. Thank goodness.

See you at the falafel stall at the old market in Jerusalem! I'll be the curly-haired American woman going on and on about the hummus at the stand right over there.

STEVEN Contemporary Israeli cuisine reflects a global consciousness rooted in a vast, mind-boggling array of cultural influences and traditions. Even the earliest inhabitants of the Land of Israel appreciated its bounty: "Let us go out early to the vineyards / and see whether the vines have budded, / whether the grape blossoms have opened / and the pomegranates are in bloom" (Song of Solomon 6:11). That bounty's importance is poignantly underscored when it is lost: "Grapevines have dried up / and so has every tree— / figs and pomegranates, date palms and apples. / All happiness has faded away" (Joel 7:12). Who can argue that fresh, raw ingredients, recipes to combine them, and the idea and act of eating do not bring us immeasurable pleasure, and add to our sense of well-being?

Each period in the land's history saw different food trends. In the earliest years, everything was locally grown. As civilization became more sophisticated, so did people's taste for food. What couldn't be sourced locally was imported from neighboring lands. The Romans, the Bedouins, and the Arab conquerors all added something unique to the earliest shopping lists. When the Crusaders showed up in the eleventh century, they fell in love with the exotic fruits and spices, and the markets they created to do their shopping are still in use in Jerusalem's Old City. The descendants of the diaspora Jews, who returned to Israel in the late nineteenth century, and the immigrants from Europe in the wake of WWII, brought the memories of their comfort foods with them. And today, after they complete their military service, young Israelis bring home flavors from their mind-bending journeys to Asia, South America, and Africa. The far-flung sources of modern Israeli cooking are as complicated as the nation's politics. Contemporary cooks in Israel are more than likely tapping into a bottomless fount of indigenous culinary traditions and practices intermingled through time by invaders, immigrants, and innovators, and are using the modern concept of fusion as their jumping off point. Right now, you can eat a black pizza whose crust is stained with squid ink, taste a sheep's milk cheese that usurps the memory of your favorite Tuscan pecorinos, and feast on the simplicity of a fragrant, gently oven-roasted cauliflower that, like a gift, is brought to the table wrapped in parchment paper.

"Do you have relevance here?" Eli, the pensive olive harvester, asked me as he squatted on a black mesh cloth, knee-deep in a carpet of Syrian olives during the harvest in Clil. Being of a contemplative nature myself, I began to turn his provocative question over in mind. Despite having grown up without a strong emphasis on religious concerns, I possess a quizzical approach to my spiritual life. I search for a deeper meaning that transcends the seductive material world that I have spent most of my life exploring through the viewfinder of my camera. Photography gives me the opportunity to search, pause, and observe. Maybe it is a landscape, the eyes of a stranger, or the way tomatoes are lined up in a market that hint at an essential otherworldliness that feeds my hungry spirit. The intensity of this place, the whiff of danger, the close physical proximity to powerful legends that reverberate across our collective unconscious is thrilling and compelling. I am a part of it because of who my ancestors were and because I am a human being, a visual anthropologist who is drawn to anything that has the mark of a human hand in it. So I told Eli that yes, I did have relevance here. He looked at me with a furrowed brow and a sheepish smile spread across his smooth face. "Sorry," he grinned, "I meant relatives. Do you have relatives here?"

My quest as a photographer and traveler has been to find good food, interesting people, and alluring places. I am in search of the element of surprise in my travels, so this is not an orthodox cookbook. There is not a symmetrical distribution of appetizers, main dishes, and desserts. I did not begin with a list of what I expected to find. I let it find me. I began my research on the ground, sniffing around, talking to people who told me about other people, who called their friends to tell them about what I was doing. I zigzagged north and south and east and west and appeared at the door and asked the chef or cook or baker or cheese maker what he or she wanted to prepare for me. This cuisine is a vivid reflection of the kaleidoscopic culture of this county. It is unique and could only be here, now.

How do you sell a destination that is mired in conflict and perceived as a dangerous place? Why not try to use the danger aspect as its selling point? Try to appeal to the kind of traveler who is looking for an adventure, willing to take a measured risk, following a pilgrim's path that has been trodden for centuries but is actually less crowded now because of the conflict and is probably less dangerous than walking through almost any American city. The travel agencies are looking for an angle—pairing it with other destinations like Rome, Istanbul, and Amsterdam, which, to me, is an injustice. Israel is a stand-alone experience; it does not need to be packaged with a Roman holiday. (Plus, seeing the Romans depicted on the Arch of Titus carrying off the temple treasures when they sacked Jerusalem in AD 70 might tarnish the appeal of the Eternal City.) The frisson of asking UN Security forces I come upon standing on a hilltop, "What are you doing here?" and having them answer, "We are observing the civil war in Syria," after I had just visited a bakery five minutes from the border is an experience that any jaded adventurer addicted to unusual, off-the-beaten-path experiences would trade his soul for.

Souls divided. And cities and churches and synagogues and mosques and men and women and Jews and Arabs and Muslims and Druze and Christians and meat and fish and dairy and markets and roads and yet and yet and yet.

Does a country more confusing and more complicated exist or has one ever existed? Moments that sped by me: the father and son praying side by side on the stairs of their house, their faces bathed in the last rays of afternoon light in Safed; the Arab woman in a blue scarf floating past an arched opening with a blue tarp above it in Akko; the young rabbi with the scraggly beard at the Ethiopian's bar mitzvah in front of the Western Wall; the French Resistance hero Marie-Rose Gineste's bicycle dangling from the ceiling at Yad Vashem; the *payot* swinging as the orthodox yeshiva students hold down their hats and run to catch a bus; the lined faces of the men smoking hookahs in the centuries-old cafe in East Jerusalem; the packed hummuseria full of soldiers laughing and eating; the young, young beautiful female soldier who, when I ask her if the road to Masada is safe at night responds, "That's what we're here for"; the police van with the flashing blue lights that comes up behind me and as it passes, the cop in the kipa flashes me a friendly smile; the holy men in fur hats and striped silk coats solemnly gliding through the streets of Meah She'arim like the Queen of Sheba and King Solomon in Piero della Francesca's frescoes, while the bartender sings along with the song blaring in the restaurant a few blocks away; the pomegranate orchards, stands of palm trees, rows of cotton, flower vendors on the highways, boys in the markets with huge wooden boxes of pita effortlessly balanced on their heads. The spiritual is palpable in everything I see.

I love the intensity of the place, the hint of danger, and the notion that so many monumental events have occurred in these landscapes. The proximity to powerful legends is thrilling and compelling. The Sea of Galilee, or Kinneret, as the Jews call it, is a mythical place. I visit the seaside village where St. Peter lived and realize that he was a simple fisherman. The eponymous church in Rome seems far removed from who he was and where he came from. Remembering the way the story of Jesus is told by Kazantzakis, the story of a people with a fervent, transcendent belief rebelling against oppression and pagan ideology, consolidating the spiritual into one thought—it all seems to make sense. Then and now, Israel is a place where people like you and me are trying to live their lives against the backdrop of dramatic events that are out of their control. Knowing the history of the Jews, it is amazing and moving that the country of Israel even exists, and seeing it for myself confirms my belief that it must continue to thrive for the sake of the warm, creative, and talented people who live there.

If you ask me where I'm going and I say France or Italy, you have a romantic, nostalgic yearning and immediately a picture comes to mind of an experience you had, a wine you tasted, a simple meal in a hilltop village, a wrong turn that led to an unforgettable discovery, the lingering scent of perfume in the metro, a rich and creamy cappuccino; but if I say Israel, what image is conjured up in your mind? Read on.

A NEW CUISINE

RONIT VERED

I met the sommelier Aviram Katz at Brut, the wine bar and restaurant he co-owns in Tel Aviv—a place, as someone described it, where cooks cook for cooks. Aviram is young and serious, dark-haired and bearded, and resembles a bohemian from nineteenth-century Paris. He gave me the names of people he thought I would enjoy meeting and spontaneously invited me to a celebration of artisan food producers in Nazareth hosted by Ronit Vered, the Haaretz journalist who wrote about them in her column "Pleasure Hunting." I had an appointment to work with another chef on the same day, but my instincts told me that this was an opportunity too interesting to pass up. On the appointed date, I entered the courtyard of the historic Fauzi Azar Inn and came face to face with the sacred and the profane. Was I in the middle of a witches' coven, or was I witnessing the Epiphany itself? Impassioned cooks materialized from all corners of Israel, bearing breads and cheese and ice creams and chocolates and meats and smoked fish and bowls of hummus and more salads than I had ever seen congregated in one place. Many of these people I had already met, and many would become the focus of my ensuing travels as this book revealed itself to me. I dined with Ronit a few times throughout the year I spent on this project and was impressed with her uncanny knowledge about the Israeli food scene. I am honored to present Ronit's brief history of food in Israel.

In 1955, seven years after the Israeli state was declared, the heads of the fledgling government decided that all families in the newly formed nation should serve a standard, prescribed menu at the annual Independence Day celebrations, similar in spirit to the traditional Passover

LUNCH AT AZURA IN JERUSALEM.

16

Seder. The Education Ministry's Department of Nutrition came up with two options for a national menu, each consisting of seven dishes, all chosen for their links to the War of Independence and evocative of the ingathering of exiles that had brought Jews to the new nation. As the first course, the menu's architects suggested patties of *hubeiza* (Arabic for "mallow") in a tomato sauce, or fresh in a salad dressed with tahini. The edible wild mallow paid homage to the siege of Jerusalem in 1948, when the Holy City was cut off from the center of the country and *hubeiza* became the locals' principal source of nourishment. Next up was a clear soup with *kreplach*, a dough stuffed with a filling that the menu's architects believed would symbolize the Jewish people's suffering during the War of Independence, just as the dough-filled pastry *hamentaschen* symbolized the defeat of Haman, an ancient enemy of the Jews, during the Purim celebration. The standardized meal would conclude with a festive dessert of Seven Species cake, inspired by the seven agricultural products—wheat, barley, grapes, figs, pomegranates, olives, and dates—that were the staples in the diet of the Jewish people in the Land of Israel during biblical times.

The Israeli state's attempt to dictate a template for uniform national celebrations was a resounding failure. Individualism triumphed over the state's attempt to dictate what people ate. Over time, Israel's Independence Day evolved naturally, and the popular celebration of the day became synonymous with the outdoors, initially picnics and later social events centering around barbequing meat in the open air. Yet the original proposal, kept in the National Library's archives, illustrates many of the defining dishes that the country's leaders hoped to instill in the earliest version of the Israeli kitchen, and documents their efforts to create fixed, shared patterns that could be considered a national kitchen in a young heterogeneous society lacking any tradition.

Discussing culinary matters was considered taboo during Israel's first two decades. In the nascent Israeli ethos, meals weren't meant, heaven forbid, to arouse enjoyment or sensual pleasure. Food was simply expected to feed the Hebrew pioneers building the new nation. The huge waves of immigration to the new country by destitute refugees from the Second World War, and migrants from Arab nations, forced to abandon all their possessions, dictated austerity and a compulsory rationing policy. Lacking their native ingredients, immigrants were unable to reconstruct traditional foods from back home, while other dishes fell into disuse because of the Israeli climate and geography, which differed from their countries of origin. In addition, both the Holocaust's aftermath and the immigration to Israel created an intergenerational divide. Young women never learned kitchen secrets from their mothers' or fathers' extended families because their recipes had been lost. The traditional domestic kitchen and the cookbooks from that era were aimed at teaching housewives how to feed a family with the meager means available rather than tips for experimenting with different local flavors. Apart from modest workers' restaurants serving spartan dishes, restaurants were few and far between.

It was only in the 1960s and 1970s, amid Israel's new prosperity, that a natural Israeli food identity put down tentative roots. At the time, many Israelis were gazing overseas; cookbooks of the period admired the American hamburger, hot and sour Chinese soup, and Italian lasagna. The distinctive Israeli fusion, known as the "melting-pot kitchen," flourished as well. Falafel is a perfect example. Native to Egypt, where it's made from fava beans, the Israeli version, influenced by the Palestinians, consists of chickpeas. Familiar with falafel, Jewish immigrants from Yemen spiced it with *hawayej*, a spice mix typical of their homeland, consisting of cumin, fenugreek, ground coriander, black pepper, cardamom, and turmeric. Another example is *sabich*, the Sabbath breakfast of Iraqi Jews, consisting of fried eggplant, hard-boiled egg, and boiled potatoes. It was popped into pita bread and, with the addition of local tahini, quickly became a definitive Israeli street food. Israeli *shawarma* resembled its original Turkish technique, but the raw ingredients were given a local twist; lamb meat was replaced by chicken or veal and spices such as turmeric, cumin, and allspice were added, thus creating the distinctive Israeli flavor that differed from the traditional Turkish version. Street food that drew inspiration from the new settlers' homelands helped integrate the Jewish arrivals into their new setting and became a major part of the local food culture. But this wasn't all. North African couscous, brought to Israel by Jewish immigrants from the Maghreb, is now served in every Israeli home, while chopped liver and schnitzel from the European-Ashkenazi heritage are regular features on the tables of Ashkenazi and Mizrahi families.

Yet Israel's real culinary revolution took off in the 1980s. The economy had stabilized and the country's increased security made it possible to enjoy leisure time and cultural pursuits, which paved the way for a lively culinary discourse. The third generation of immigrants, unscathed by the negative connotations around foreign culinary influences that had characterized their parents' and grandparents' generations, rediscovered the rich, authentic kitchens that had been abandoned in the ancestral countries. Young Israeli chefs gained expertise in Michelin-starred European restaurants, acquired professional skills, and applied modern cooking techniques to traditional recipes. In the process, they implemented the foundations of a dynamic Israeli restaurant scene that continues to attract international attention. Despite the complex political situation, the global trend toward restaurant chefs and family cooks seeking out fine-quality local materials has generated tremendous interest in the traditional Palestinian kitchen, and notably provides inspiration for a new Israeli cuisine. Olive oil, lamb, tahini, edible wild herbs, and local spices now are prominent features of Israel's emerging culinary language.

Still, a definitive definition of the "new" Israeli cuisine does not exist. The emerging Israeli cuisine is growing vigorously, and the absence of centuries-old rigid and restrictive traditions has proved to be beneficial for Israeli chefs. These chefs have the freedom to create an innovative and daring culinary world. The new Israeli kitchen takes it inspiration from the Mediterranean, from the Middle East, from the history of the Land of Israel, from the Roman Empire to the Ottoman Empire, from the two millennia of Jewish exile, and from the ethnic and religious minorities living in the modern state. Adding to this vast cultural assortment is the geographic diversity. Though a small country, Israel has diverse regions differing in climate and terroir, from the mountainous north through the coastal cities of the central region and down to the arid desert regions in the south, all offering an inspiring range of high-quality ingredients.

While there might not be a fully encompassing, accurate, or even agreed-upon definition of Israeli Cuisine, any hungry traveler who bites into an eggplant grilled over charcoal with sunshine-toned olive oil and tahini, a beautifully braided little marzipan *challah*, a chicken roasted with pickled lemons and *harissa*, or a ceviche of a Mediterranean fish with *Arak* and baladi tomatoes (a locally grown species) will rapidly become familiar with the singular language of the New Israeli Cuisine.

TEL AVIV–JAFFA

THE LOUD WHACKS OF THE SMALL RUBBER BALLS hitting the wooden paddles of the Matkot players on the beachfront drown out the sound of the sea and underscore just how serious the Tel Avivim are about their fun. On a walk along the three-mile Tayelet boardwalk between Jaffa and the Tel Aviv port, there are hundreds of people absorbed in this game that has no rules, no winners, and no losers. It is played just for the fun of it. This reveals a lot about life in Tel Aviv. The 300 sunny days a year make it an ideal place to find pleasure, and eating is one of the most important pursuits. If you walk along Rothschild Boulevard among the other flaneurs, you will find a wide selection of drinks and snacks to choose from in the open-air kiosks that line the street. Add to this all the other boulevards with cafés, restaurants, and kiosks, throw in the Carmel, Levinsky, and Ha Tikva markets, and the Farmers Market at the port, and you will never have to travel more than a few steps to find sustenance. Clearly, food is as serious an interest as fun in Tel Aviv, often dubbed The City That Never Sleeps and ranked the second-most innovative city in the world by the *Wall Street Journal* in 2013. Why waste time sleeping when you can eat, play, and innovate?

Eyal Shani, owner of North Abraxas restaurant, never misses an opportunity to talk about his importance as an innovator. "I was the first Israeli to use olive oil in cooking, the first to create my own olive oil, the first to discover focaccia, the first to do a carpaccio of fish, the first to use lamb, and the first in the world to do vegetable sashimi," he states with aplomb. Inarguably, Eyal has contributed a great deal to modern Israeli cuisine, and along the way has forged a controversial persona. He told me, "Israelis are wise and clever, and learn quickly. They have no roots and are very flexible and lightweight." His hubris shines a light on his unorthodox approach to the revered cauliflower, which, he believes, "is not a flower, but a small animal in the same shape as a brain." After blanching the cauliflower, Eyal believes the big question is how much oil it takes to roast it in a brick oven so that it will come out golden brown. Not enough oil will make it dry and too much will fry it. His solution? "Take two hands covered in oil and rub the cauliflower like you are rubbing the head of a baby or a dog." However strange his method and ideology might sound, the simple and pure result, delivered whole to the table on a piece of parchment paper with a pinch of sea salt tossed next to it, is true perfection.

Serious fun overflowed in the North Abraxas kitchen when I spent the day there. Midway through lunch, a cook lit a bowl of fresh herbs on fire, and as the smoke wafted through the restaurant, the six-foot-five-inch barman lifted the five-foot Eretrean cook off the ground in a tight embrace. When I asked the taller man if he was cracking the smaller man's back, he replied, "No, I just love him." Chef de cuisine Tal Zion Kawi told me, "This is a different kitchen, not strict, with a lot of freedom to create. Eyal gives us the language and then we speak." This symbiosis between Eyal and his protégés has served the restaurant well. It bursts with energy, and for years customers have been waiting in long lines to eat unusual food in the rarefied atmosphere.

Pleasure is an integral aspect of celebrity chef Meir Adoni's culinary philosophy as well, and there is very little that can stop him from delivering it to the masses. Meir, the owner of four popular restaurants and the creator of gourmet fast food sold in gas stations, told me that when someone tastes his food, he wants it to "scratch their mind and kick their mouth; their brain must scream from happiness." During the 2014 military operation in Gaza, when many restaurants in Tel Aviv were empty, Meir took his chefs to the border to cook for the soldiers. Despite the challenges of fighting a war, there was little doubt that his innovative cuisine elicited the strong emotional responses he described to me and uplifted the spirits of the soldiers, who were being fed star-chef food in a tragic atmosphere.

In Israel, it is difficult to separate pleasure and pain because the tension between the two always seems to be lurking beneath the surface, yet the people I met during my travels were predominantly optimistic. Chef Asaf Doktor, owner of Haachim, said, "Israel is not only about Bibi and wars; it is about a new generation finding itself through its culture and its food." Haachim pays homage to an Arab concept from the 1970s called a *shipudia*, a restaurant that specialized in skewered meats cooked on a charcoal grill. Asaf's fond memories of Shipudia Olga, a place he loved when he was growing up in Caesarea, provide the inspiration for his restaurant, but he serves different dishes and uses only fresh local products. He pulls ideas from the memories of his past and weaves them into the culture and future of his own hopeful generation.

If I were to pick a food trend that best represents this new generation of Israelis inventing their own culture of food, the strongest contender would be veganism. The American website *The Daily Meal* named Tel Aviv the top destination in the world for vegan travelers in 2015, and rated Harel Zakaim's restaurant, Zakaim, number twenty on the list of the top twenty-five vegan restaurants in the world. Harel believes that the American animal rights activist Gary Yourofsky is responsible for converting many Israelis to veganism after a speech he made in 2010 at Georgia Tech was recorded, subtitled in Hebrew, and posted on YouTube. Over a million Israelis have watched it, and it has become the most-viewed speech in the country's history, with approximately one in seven people having seen it. Harel and his sisters Hani and Hila, who are his partners in the restaurant, want to bring a "quiet" veganism to their customers, sixty percent of whom are non-vegan. "The Israeli kitchen is the widest in the world. Jews from all over brought their heritages and memories together in one place, and the variety of farm products is so enormous that we can build a kitchen from only local fruits and vegetables and it too will be very wide." Salt is the only ingredient Harel uses that is not local.

The food blogger Oz Telem contacted me after he read about my progress on this book in the online food magazine *Walla*. Oz told me he was excited to hear that someone was undertaking such an important project, and he said he wanted to contribute to it in some way. I asked him if he would like to share a few recipes and prepare them for me to photograph, and he immediately agreed. We met a few months later and spent a morning working together and talking about his serendipitous career path.

Before Oz figured out that cooking would be the main source of pleasure and satisfaction in his life, he had felt precariously adrift. His search for a new direction encouraged him to answer a call for contestants on the reality show *Beauty and the Geek*. He was eliminated after a disastrous date in a villa in the southern city of Eilat, and this disappointing experience became a catalyst to look deeper into his life, "like going to India to find myself without going to India." He began practicing yoga, and his instructor told him his heart chakra was closed and he needed to look for a new path that would give him the opportunity to do the things he loved. Looking inward, Oz realized, "I had been cooking since I could remember myself," and he had the epiphany that the food world was where he belonged. He started taking cooking classes while studying business in college and discovered that everything

he did in the kitchen had a purpose and meaning. "Behind even the simplest dish," he muses, "there is history, culture, heritage, biology, and physics—in short, an endless gold mine of infinite knowledge." Oz's life has probably been more satisfying than it would have been had his first date with the Beauty been a success. He has become a recipe developer for a number of industrial food companies, the writer of two weekly columns about the history of food and practical kitchen food support, and the creator of the popular blog *The Kitchen Coach*, which has inspired thousands of Israelis to cook more adventurously at home.

My experience with Oz Telem was one of a handful of enlightening connections I made with people in Israel whose lives have been enhanced by their relationship to food. Few stories I heard, however, possessed the improbable combination of events that have defined the trajectory of Tom Franz's life.

When Tom was in high school in his native Germany in the late 1980s, he befriended the Israeli exchange students who were studying at his school. For reasons he could not pinpoint, there was a mutual affection between the German native and the foreign visitors. In 1990, when he was sixteen years old, he went to Israel on the same exchange program that had brought the Israelis to Germany, and he felt completely at home in the country. He finished the year, returned to Germany, and kept in touch with his Israeli friends for the next three years.

The friendships eventually faded, but his love for the country endured. He returned five years later with Action Reconciliation Service for Peace, a German organization that sends young volunteers to work with survivors in countries terrorized by the Nazis during WWII. For eighteen months, he worked in hospitals, visited German Holocaust survivors, and learned colloquial Hebrew. He had earned his degree in banking before he left Germany, and after his commitment ended in Israel, he returned home to study law. He completed his degree, practiced with an international firm, and when he turned thirty, faced an existential crisis. Tom examined his priorities and realized that his law career was not as important to him as his longing for Israel, Judaism, and a spiritual life that embraced marriage and a family. In the winter of 2004, he arrived in Israel on a tourist visa and decided that he would spend the rest of his life there. He fought with the Ministry of Internal Affairs for eighteen months until they agreed to let him stay and convert, but he was not allowed to work. His life was difficult, but he was happy. He told me, "When I have an aim, I really go for it," and within two and a half years, he was Jewish. As a Jew, he was given the right to make aliya—legally immigrate—and become an Israeli citizen.

During his first year living in Israel as an observant Jewish man who kept kosher, Tom saw Dana Hadari sitting on a bench across from a juice bar on Yirmiyahu Street and wanted to meet her. When I asked Dana what her first impression of Tom was, she said, "I thought to myself, who is this tall, handsome guy walking back and forth? Come talk to me! (I thought it but didn't say it.)" She was not particularly religious, but she had started dressing modestly, observing Shabbat, and keeping kosher. He cooked for her on their first few dates, and his talent overwhelmed her. "How do you know how to cook this way?" Dana asked him, and even though Tom was practicing law on a freelance basis, she was convinced that he should develop his skills as a chef. Two years after they met, they were married, and when the *Master Chef* television show began its first season, Dana encouraged him to try

out for the next season's competition. The birth of their son and Dana's unexpected illness prevented him from trying out for the second season, but when the third season began, she made sure that he prepared himself for the challenge. He was as focused and intense about studying cooking as he had been about banking, law, and becoming Jewish. He studied for eight hours a day and practiced in the kitchen for three. When Tom made it on to the show, he was an instant hit with the Israeli public. The finale of his *Master Chef* season was the highest-rated single TV episode in Israeli history, and the most-watched reality TV finale ever, with fifty-two percent of all Jewish households tuned in. Tom's triumph elevated the Israeli public's appreciation of kosher food and, he wryly suggested, gave them "a slightly better opinion of Germans."

As Tom recounted his story, the surreal aspect of a few million Jews all sitting in their homes simultaneously spellbound by the story of a convert from Germany competing on an Israeli cooking show was not lost on me. Given the many supernatural events recorded as having happened there, being in Israel lends itself to frequent dreamlike experiences.

On a hot, clear spring evening, Nancy and I met Eitan and Ariela Wertheimer at their soaring aerie above the city. The panoramic views of the sea and the skyline made my knees wobble and gave me a comprehensive understanding of Tel Aviv's topology. We had plans to have dinner at Yonatan Roshfeld's Herbert Samuel restaurant, one of the pillars of Tel Aviv's culinary landscape. As we descended from their home to the street below, Eitan herded us around the corner for an appetizer or two at Popina, a restaurant nearby, where I had dined with the Wertheimers and some of their friends on my previous visit. I liked the idea because chef Orel Kimchi served a black squid ink pizza that I knew Nancy would love. A few pizzas, shrimp burgers, and glasses of champagne later, we were off to Herbert Samuel for dinner. We tasted grilled asparagus with cauliflower cream, a Jerusalem artichoke soup, blue crabs with oregano and fresh lime, and yellowtail with roasted eggplant. Somehow the conversation turned to food, and Eitan thought we should try a few dishes at Shila, the restaurant named after chef Sharon Cohen's dog. At a few minutes before midnight, we were sitting at a generously proportioned square bar, eating our third dinner. At this point, my taste buds were in a state of siege and I don't remember what we ate. When the kitchen closed, I was relieved to be done with food and longed to stroll through the city that was still awake.

We stepped out into the warm night air, and Eitan and Ariela gave us an early morning architectural tour, pointing out some of the interesting buildings that surrounded us. We sat down on a bench and Eitan took out his phone, held it up against the backdrop of buildings shrouded in darkness, and played a video clip of the psychologist and Holocaust survivor Viktor Frankl talking about man's search for meaning and purpose in life. My senses took in the grainy black-and-white images on the small screen, the curvy pastel Bauhaus buildings, the legs of a person running past us, and the heavily accented voice of Frankl quoting Goethe: "If we take man as he is, we make him worse, but if we take him as he should be, we make him capable of becoming what he can be."

I wondered if the same theory could be applied to a group of people or even a country. Fellini couldn't have created a more surreal atmosphere than the one I found myself in at that moment on the streets of Tel Aviv at two in the morning.

TAL ZION KAWI, CHEF AT NORTH ABRAXAS IN TEL AVIV.

Cauliflower "Tabouleh"

When Oz Telem, food writer, recipe developer, and creator of *The Kitchen Coach* blog, created this light, crunchy salad, he used as his inspiration Alton Brown's idea of cauliflower as an understudy for bulgur in tabouleh. It is a natural choice for someone who lives in a country that reveres the cauliflower, and I am hoping the idea will go global so that more people will learn to appreciate this pristine and salubrious vegetable.

1 small to medium cauliflower, divided into florets

1 large bunch parsley, leaves only, finely chopped

10 large mint sprigs, leaves only, finely chopped

3 green onions, finely chopped

¼ cup (40 g) chopped dried blueberries, cranberries, or raisins

¼ cup (60 ml) olive oil

¼ cup (60 ml) fresh lemon juice

Salt and freshly ground pepper

Place the cauliflower florets in a food processor. Pulse until small crumbs form; do not over pulse or cauliflower will become watery. Alternatively, grate cauliflower finely on a box grater. Transfer cauliflower crumbs to a large bowl. Add the parsley, mint, green onions, and blueberries. Dress with the olive oil and lemon juice; toss well. Season with salt and pepper. Serve immediately.

Braised Cabbage and Carrots with Lamb Bones

Tal Zion Kawi, the chef at North Abraxas restaurant, told me that he could eat vegetable soup every day for the rest of his life. When he revealed this innocuous truth about himself, his cuisine made perfect sense. Simplicity reigns. And what is simpler than a beautiful head of cabbage slowly cooked with lamb bones? This is hearty enough to be eaten alone, or for a fresh and tangy contrast, serve it with Nancy's Freekeh Tabouleh on page 100.

1 (4- to 5-pound; 1.8 to 2.2 kg) green cabbage
4 pounds (1.8 kg) lamb bones, preferably from shank, cut into 3- to 4-inch-long (7.6 to 10 cm) pieces
1 large carrot, coarsely chopped
Salt
Sour cream

A CABBAGE GROWN BY AVI ARAZUNI ON HIS FARM IN THE SOUTHERN VILLAGE OF EZUZ.

Preheat the oven to 300°F (150°C).

Cut a parchment paper round to fit over the top of a large ovenproof pot. Place the cabbage in the pot, surrounding it with bones and carrot pieces. Season lightly with salt. Add enough water to cover the cabbage and bring to a boil, skimming foam from the surface. Remove from heat. Cover pot with the prepared parchment paper. Bake until cabbage is very soft and the liquid is thick, about 4½ hours.

Cool cabbage slightly; transfer from the liquid to a cutting board. Cut the cabbage into chunks; transfer to bowls. Spoon some of cooking liquid over the cabbage, garnish with sour cream, and serve.

Roasted Beet Carpaccio

This Roasted Beet Carpaccio is one of the best things I have ever eaten. The long roasting at high heat creates a beetroot with a creamy texture that I like to think of as the foie gras of Mother Earth. When I asked Chef Tal Zion Kawi of North Abraxas if I would be able to make this taste as good at home, he answered, "It's not that difficult; you just have to nail it."

10 small beets, rinsed well

Extra virgin olive oil

Sea salt

4 tablespoons sour cream or
   crème fraîche

Preheat the oven to its highest setting, usually 450 to 500°F (230 to 260°C). Place the beets on a baking sheet and bake for 2½ hours; beets will look like charcoal pieces and can be easily pierced with a knife.

Cool beets completely. Discard the charred skin from the beets and thinly slice them. Divide the beet slices among four plates. Drizzle with olive oil, and then sprinkle with sea salt. Garnish each plate with 1 tablespoon sour cream and serve.

Spinach and Bulgur Salad

Sharabik (page 102) and Ezba are two cult Arab restaurants in the northern town of Rameh. Friends told me that if you are a fan of one, you don't go to the other, kind of like being loyal to a favorite soccer team. The food blogger, writer, and recipe developer Oz Telem created this simple recipe after being inspired by a salad he tasted at Ezba. The main ingredient is hubeza, a type of mallow that grows wild all over Israel and can be found in farmers markets in the United States. If you cannot find it, use wild spinach instead.

2 tablespoons olive oil

1 pound (450 g) wild spinach leaves
   (or mallow if you can find it)

Salt

4 heaping tablespoons fine
   bulgur wheat

½ lemon

Freshly ground pepper

Additional olive oil (optional)

Heat 2 tablespoons olive oil in a large heavy skillet over high heat. Add the spinach and a pinch of salt and cook until the leaves just wilt and exude some liquid, 3 to 4 minutes. Remove from heat. Add the bulgur and stir well so all grains come in contact with liquid, adding up to 1 tablespoon water if not enough liquid in skillet. Cover skillet and let stand off heat until bulgur absorbs liquid and becomes tender, 5 to 6 minutes. Squeeze the lemon half over the salad. Adjust seasoning with salt and pepper. Drizzle with additional olive oil if desired.

Beef and Lamb Siniya
with Roasted Vegetables

Siniya is the Arabic word for "pan" and is used to describe a wide range of interesting recipes. Chef Asaf Doktor, owner of Haachim, told me he cooks what he knows his clientele likes, and they come back to eat the same dishes again and again. One of his most beloved recipes is this version of siniya—beef and lamb cooked with roasted eggplant, tomatoes, and a collection of spices from the diverse array of Middle Eastern seasonings, baharat, ras el hanout, and sumac.

1 large eggplant

2 large red tomatoes

2 medium unpeeled onions

Salt and freshly ground pepper

2 pounds ground beef, not too lean

¼ pound (113 g) ground lamb fat
  or butter at room temperature

1 large onion, chopped

½ cup (20 g) plus 3 tablespoons
  chopped flat-leaf parsley

1 tablespoon baharat or ras el
  hanout

2 teaspoons salt

½ cup (120 ml) (or more) ice-cold
  water

½ cup (120 ml) (or more) tahini

3 tablespoons coarsely chopped
  roasted almonds

Ground sumac

Preheat the grill to high or the oven to 450°F (232°C).

Set the eggplant, tomatoes, and unpeeled onions on the grill or arrange on a baking sheet and place in the oven. Cook until the peels blacken and the flesh is soft, about 1 hour. Let the vegetables cool.

When vegetables are cool, peel them. Coarsely chop each vegetable and place in a bowl. Toss to mix. Transfer chopped vegetables to a 10-inch (25 cm) round pan, spreading evenly. Season with salt and pepper.

Place the beef in a large bowl. Add the fat or butter, onion, ½ cup (20 g) parsley, spice, and 2 teaspoons salt. Using clean hands, mix the meat gently but thoroughly, and make golf ball–size patties, flattening slightly.

Preheat the grill to medium or place a cast-iron skillet over medium heat. Arrange the patties on the grill or in the skillet and cook to desired degree of doneness. Transfer patties to a cutting board and coarsely chop. Spread the meat over the roasted vegetables.

Preheat the oven to 300°F (149°C).

Pour the water and tahini in a bowl and whisk until smooth and white; the consistency should be like thick yogurt. If too thin, add more tahini; if too thick, add more water. Season with salt. Pour the tahini over the meat and vegetables. Bake until tahini is set and golden brown and siniya is heated all the way through, 30 to 45 minutes. Garnish with the remaining 3 tablespoons parsley, almonds, and sumac. Serve immediately.

DINERS AT HAACHIM.

Pink Trout with Fried Smashed Potatoes, Horseradish Cream, Mustard Vinaigrette, and Green Beans

4 SERVINGS

When Nancy and I ate lunch at Ran Shmueli's restaurant, Claro, she had difficulty focusing on what we were eating because whenever a server whisked by us with a gorgeous plate of food, she said longingly, "I want what everyone else is having." We both agreed that this layered dish of cold-smoked fresh trout—a *salade niçoise* with an identity crisis—was a triumphant success in the blending of texture, flavor, and color. The chef cold smokes the trout before he sautés it. If you would like to do that as well, please see the note at the end of the recipe.

HORSERADISH CREAM

½ cup (115 g) sour cream

½ cup (120 g) strained yogurt or labneh

2 tablespoons grated fresh horseradish

1 teaspoon salt

MUSTARD VINAIGRETTE

2 tablespoons coarse grain mustard

1 tablespoon honey

½ teaspoon salt

¼ cup (60 ml) extra virgin olive oil

¼ cup (60 ml) vegetable oil

POTATOES

1 pound (450 g) kosher salt

2 pounds (900 g) baby potatoes

Vegetable oil (for deep-frying)

Salt and freshly ground pepper

FOR CREAM: Combine all the ingredients in a bowl and whisk to blend. Cover and refrigerate until ready to use.

FOR VINAIGRETTE: Whisk the mustard, honey, and salt in a bowl. Whisk in both oils in a steady stream and continue whisking until emulsified. Let stand until ready to use, re-whisking before use.

FOR POTATOES: Preheat the oven to 350°F (175°C).

Spread the salt in a roasting pan. Nestle the potatoes in salt. Bake until potatoes are tender, about 40 minutes; the baking time will vary depending on the size of potatoes. Let potatoes cool. When cool, crush each potato with the palm of your hand.

Heat the oil to 375°F (190°C) in a large heavy pot or deep fryer. Add potatoes to oil (in batches; do not crowd) and fry until golden and crisp, about 5 minutes. Transfer potatoes from oil to paper towels to drain. Season with salt and pepper. Keep potatoes warm.

FISH

1 tablespoon olive oil

4 skin-on pink trout or thin wild
salmon fillets

SERVICE

½ pound (230 g) haricots verts or
thin string beans, blanched and
cut into 1-inch (2.5 cm) pieces

2 green onions, chopped

1 bunch watercress

FOR FISH AND GARNISH: Heat the oil in a large heavy skillet over medium heat. Add the fish fillets skin-side down and cook for 5 minutes; do not turn over.

FOR SERVICE: Spread some mustard vinaigrette on each of four plates. Arrange the potatoes atop the vinaigrette. Spoon the horseradish cream over potatoes. Set fish fillet atop potatoes. Garnish with green beans, onions, and watercress.

To cold smoke fish:

Line the bottom of a 9 x 13-inch (23 x 33 cm) glass baking dish with fresh thyme and rosemary sprigs. Set a metal baking or cooling rack in the dish atop the herbs. Arrange the fish fillets on the rack. Light the herbs on fire, then immediately blow the fire out, creating smoke. Cover the baking dish with foil. Set in a cold oven for 20 minutes, and then proceed with recipe.

Nancy's Whole Roasted Cauliflower with Za'atar and Mint Yogurt Sauce

The first thing I noticed when I walked into North Abraxas in Tel Aviv was an entire cupboard filled with whole roasted cauliflowers resting on parchment paper. It was an unexpected decoration, even though a friend who visited Chef Eyal Shani's restaurant in Paris forewarned me that he was big time into cauliflower. I am a huge fan of cauliflower but have only had it cut up into florets or as a baby. Here, they were the size of volleyballs. This was the most audacious display of cauliflower I had ever seen. And they were delicious. At Pizzeria Mozza, I have included the cauliflower in our new roasted vegetable program. This is how we serve it there.

2 whole cauliflowers with green leaves attached

Extra virgin olive oil (for rubbing cauliflowers)

2 tablespoons za'atar (page 91)

1 cup (245 g) whole milk Greek yogurt, but not an overly thick brand

2 tablespoons extra virgin olive oil

1 tablespoon fresh lemon juice

2 to 3 medium garlic cloves, minced

$1/2$ teaspoon kosher salt

$1/2$ cup (20 g) packed whole mint leaves, finely chopped (about $1/4$ cup)

Freshly ground pepper

Preheat the oven to its highest setting, usually 450 to 500°F (230 to 260°C). Bring a large pot of heavily salted water to a boil. Add the cauliflowers and blanch for 6 minutes. Meanwhile, prepare a large bowl of ice water. Remove cauliflowers from the boiling water and submerge them in ice water to stop the cooking process.

When cauliflowers are cool, remove from the ice water and pat dry with paper towels. Set on baking sheets or in a baking pan and massage generously with olive oil, making sure that the oil seeps into all the crevices of the cauliflowers, especially the centers. Roast cauliflowers until they are browned, rotating the pan for even browning, 15 to 20 minutes. Sprinkle the cauliflowers with za'atar.

Place the yogurt in a bowl. Add the oil, lemon juice, garlic, and salt and stir well. Using a spatula, fold in the mint. Season with pepper. Serve cauliflowers whole with yogurt sauce.

PREVIOUS OVERLEAF: THE KITCHEN AT NORTH ABRAXAS.

Nancy's Whole Roasted Carrots with Cracked Coriander and Dill Crème Fraîche

2 SIDE-DISH SERVINGS

My vegetable awakening journey continued at Ran Shmueli's restaurant, Claro. When I walked into the tasteful modern space, I was greeted by a large wooden table laden with an array of vegetables, many of them roasted whole. There was a gigantic squash being cut into serving portions as if it were a twenty-pound ham. Next to it were whole heads of broccoli, and off to one side were whole roasted large carrots. I have always been a fan of roasted carrots. One of the most popular items on the Pizzeria Mozza menu is the plate of small, roasted farmers market carrots. We roast them for ten to fifteen minutes at a high temperature, but these large whole carrots, because of their girth, roast for forty minutes. The long cooking time not only brings the sweetness to the outside by caramelizing them, it also gives the center a creamy consistency. My favorite seasonings for carrots are cumin, coriander, and fresh dill.

6 extra-large carrots

Extra virgin olive oil

Kosher salt

2 tablespoons coriander seeds

2 tablespoons cumin seeds

1/2 cup (5 g) plus 2 tablespoons chopped dill

2 cups (460 g) crème fraîche

2 tablespoons fresh lemon juice

Preheat the oven to its highest setting, usually 450 to 500°F (230 to 260°C).

Rub the carrots with olive oil and season with salt. Arrange carrots on a baking sheet or in a small roasting pan. Roast carrots, shaking the pan occasionally, until they are tender and charred in places, about 40 minutes; the roasting time will vary depending on the size of the carrots.

Meanwhile, place the coriander seeds in a heavy small skillet and stir over medium heat until fragrant; transfer to a bowl. Add the cumin seeds to the same skillet and stir over medium heat until fragrant; transfer to the same bowl. Let cool. Transfer the seeds to a mortar and grind with a pestle until just cracked. Alternatively, place seeds in a spice grinder and pulse until just cracked. Sprinkle cracked spices and 2 tablespoons chopped dill on the carrots and toss to coat.

Combine the crème fraîche and lemon juice in a small bowl. Stir in the remaining 1/2 cup chopped dill. Serve with the roasted carrots.

Charred Eggplant
with Spicy Tomato Sauce

"Spicy is happy and sweet is comfort," Harel Zakaim told me as I put a forkful of this peppery eggplant into my mouth at his vegan restaurant, Zakaim. His decision to be vegan is grounded less in the desire be healthy than it is in the desire to be happy. "Being vegan is something to talk about with friends who refuse to talk about politics," he says, and "cooking is the best way I know of to communicate." Don't forget to serve challah with this life-affirming dish.

1 small globe eggplant

2 tablespoons olive oil

1 large green chili, sliced

4 large garlic cloves, coarsely chopped

1/2 pound (230 g) tomatoes, coarsely chopped

Salt

Tahini

Green chilies, minced

Cook the eggplant on all sides over a high open flame until the skin is charred and the flesh is cooked but still firm (use tongs or place eggplant on a metal skewer). Let cool to the touch, then peel off skin from eggplant. Slice eggplant into a fan, leaving stem intact.

Preheat the broiler. Heat the oil in a heavy medium skillet over medium heat. Add the sliced chili and sauté until golden around the edges, about 1 minute; stand back, as oil may splatter on initial contact with chili. Add the garlic and sauté until fragrant, about 1 minute. Add the tomatoes, season with salt, and let stand 1 minute without stirring, then cook until a thick sauce forms, stirring frequently, about 5 minutes.

Dip both sides of eggplant into sauce. Transfer sauce to an ovenproof baking dish. Arrange eggplant atop sauce. Broil until eggplant is scorched, 10 to 15 minutes. Garnish with tahini and minced chilies and serve immediately.

Roasted Assorted Vegetables with Garlic, Lemon, and Herbs

Ran Shmueli, the owner of Claro, is very serious about his vegetables. Every month a different vegetable is chosen as the star, and he prepares the featured vegetable differently each time. Ran has a deep reverence for what grows in the ground and told me that he spends almost as much on vegetables as he does on seafood and meat. When I asked him which vegetable was the biggest diva, he unhesitatingly replied, "the turnip."

This recipe is cooked in a wood-burning oven at the restaurant, but a hot kitchen oven will also work well. Use the best and the freshest vegetables and olive oil you can find and improvise with what is in season. Feel free to select whatever seasonal vegetables appeal to you.

1 small red cabbage, cut
   into wedges

2 medium onions, peeled

Salt

4 young carrots

2 medium turnips

4 medium beets

2 medium red bell peppers

2 medium yellow bell peppers

2 firm medium tomatoes, halved

1 medium eggplant, cut into
   chunks

4 green onions

1/2 large head garlic

Extra virgin olive oil

Sea salt

2 lemons, halved

Chopped parsley

Chopped oregano

RECIPE PICTURED ON PAGE 3.

Place the cabbage and onions in a pot. Add enough water to cover. Add salt and bring to a boil. Immediately remove from heat and let stand in water for 15 minutes. Transfer cabbage and onions to a large roasting pan. Reserve the cooking water.

Place the carrots and turnips in one pot and the beets in another pot. Add enough water to cover and bring to a boil. Reduce the heat and simmer until the vegetables are almost tender. Transfer vegetables to roasting pan with cabbage and onions. Reserve the carrot and turnip cooking water. Discard the beet cooking water.

Add the peppers, tomatoes, and eggplant to the roasting pan with the other vegetables. Add the green onions and garlic.

Preheat the oven to its highest setting, usually 450 to 500°F (230 to 260°C). Combine all reserved cooking water in one large pot and boil it until it is reduced by a fifth. Pour the reduced cooking water over the vegetables in the roasting pan. Drizzle with olive oil and sprinkle with sea salt. Roast in oven until all vegetables are tender.

Adjust seasoning with additional olive oil and salt. Squeeze the lemons over the vegetables. Garnish with parsley and oregano and serve.

Baked Sweet Potato Bites with Avocado, Lemon, Onion, and Chili

5 BITES OR 1 SERVING

Harel Zakaim, the chef and owner of the eponymous vegan restaurant Zakaim, calls this combination of sweet potato and avocado his version of sashimi. Each bite is packed with bursts of flavor and textures that will surprise and please every palate. Serve them as an hors d'oeuvre with a flute of crisp champagne and your omnivorous and vegan friends will fight over the last one.

1 small sweet potato

1 small ripe avocado

1 small lemon, halved, one half thinly sliced

1 small onion, very thinly sliced

1 small fresh green chili, very thinly sliced

Extra virgin olive oil

Salt and freshly ground pepper

Preheat the oven to 450°F (230°C).

Place the sweet potato on a tray and bake until soft, about 20 minutes. Let cool.

Peel the avocado. Spoon out 5 bite-size chunks and place them flat-side down on a serving plate.

Peel the sweet potato. Spoon out 5 bite-size chunks and place them atop the avocado chunks. Top each layer of avocado and sweet potato with a thin slice of lemon, a thin slice of onion, and a thin slice of chili. Squeeze the lemon half over all. Drizzle with olive oil and season with salt and pepper. Serve.

Mushroom Falafel with Herb Tabouleh and Sweet and Spicy Yogurt Sauce

Some might ask, "Why gild the lily and alter the perfectly realized falafel?" Yet just one bite of Master Chef Tom Franz's mushroom version convinced me to reconsider the traditional falafel. Not abandon it, just open my mind to the earthy mushroom taste and crisp exterior of these rebels. Tom makes an ironclad case with his accompanying fresh yogurt sauce and fragrant tabouleh.

YOGURT SAUCE

¾ cup (180 ml) Greek yogurt

¾ cup (180 ml) sour cream

2 teaspoons honey

1 small fresh chili, finely chopped

Salt and freshly ground pepper

TABOULEH

1 cup (140 g) fine bulgur

2 cups (475 ml) boiling water

2 cups (110 g) minced parsley

2 cups (110 g) minced cilantro

½ cup (60 g) minced mint

3 tablespoons extra virgin olive oil

1 tablespoon fresh lemon juice

Salt and freshly ground pepper

Additional olive oil and lemon juice

FALAFEL

3½ tablespoons butter

1 medium onion, finely chopped

Salt and freshly ground pepper

3 garlic cloves, chopped

1 pound 6 ounces (600 g) button
   mushrooms, chopped

3½ ounces (100 g) cream cheese,
   room temperature

1 generous cup (100 g) grated
   Parmesan cheese

(continued)

FOR SAUCE: Combine all the ingredients in a bowl. Let stand for at least 2 hours at room temperature before serving.

FOR TABOULEH: Place the bulgur in a bowl. Pour the boiling water over it and stir once. Let stand until liquid is absorbed, 15 to 20 minutes.

Add the parsley, cilantro, mint, 3 tablespoons olive oil, and 1 tablespoon lemon juice to bulgur and mix well. Season with salt and pepper. Add additional olive oil and lemon juice if desired. Let stand until ready to use.

FOR FALAFEL: Melt the butter in a large heavy skillet. Add the onion and sauté until golden brown, about 10 minutes. Season with salt and pepper. Stir in the garlic. Add the mushrooms and cook, stirring occasionally until they are soft and their liquid has been exuded and reabsorbed, about 10 minutes. Season with salt and pepper. Transfer the mushroom mixture to a bowl and let cool to room temperature.

Add both cheeses, 1 tablespoon flour, and the nutmeg to the mushrooms and stir to blend well. Season with salt and pepper.

Heat the oil to 375°F (190°C) in a large heavy pot or deep fryer.

Pour additional flour into a shallow bowl. Crack the egg into a second shallow bowl and beat to blend. Pour the breadcrumbs into another shallow bowl. Roll the mushroom mixture into walnut-size balls. Dredge a ball in the flour bowl, shaking off any excess; dip in egg, allowing any excess to drip back into the bowl, and dredge in breadcrumbs, shaking off any excess. Add the ball to the hot oil and fry until golden brown, 3 to 5 minutes. Repeat until all the mushroom balls are fried.

1 tablespoon all-purpose flour

¼ teaspoon grated nutmeg

Canola oil (for deep-frying)

Additional all-purpose flour (for
  dredging)

1 egg

Panko breadcrumbs (for dredging)

OVERLEAF: WATCHING THE SUNSET
FROM THE TAYELET BOARDWALK.

Using a slotted utensil, transfer the falafels to a plate. Keep
them warm in a low oven.

TO SERVE: Mound the tabouleh on a platter. Arrange the falafels
atop tabouleh. Serve with yogurt sauce.

Fried Potatoes with Homemade Ketchup and Avocado Aïoli

2 SERVINGS

When I met Harel Zakaim at his vegan restaurant Zakaim, we sat together at a table outside and discussed what he would prepare for me to photograph. He poured us tall glasses of fresh lemonade and, about a half hour later, announced that he was hungry and ordered some food. After more than two hours of talking and tasting almost everything on his menu, he looked at me with a shocked expression and said, "I never eat with guests." I laughed and told him that I never eat when I work either, and dipped another hot, crispy, soft potato chunk into the avocado aïoli. During the months that I worked on this book, I learned that Israelis love to talk for hours, and whenever possible, at a table where food is being served.

3 medium baking potatoes

9 tablespoons extra virgin olive oil, divided

1 fresh green chili, sliced

4 large garlic cloves, coarsely chopped

½ pound (230 g) tomatoes, coarsely chopped

Coarse salt

1 tablespoon apple cider vinegar

1 medium-size ripe avocado

3 tablespoons fresh lemon juice

1 large garlic clove, peeled

1 green onion, chopped

Vegetable oil (for deep-frying)

Preheat the oven to 450°F (230°C).

Place the potatoes directly on the oven floor and bake until soft but not mushy, about 20 minutes; cooking time will vary depending on the size of potatoes. Let potatoes cool.

Heat 4 tablespoons olive oil in a large heavy skillet over medium-high heat. Add the chili and sauté until golden around the edges, about 3 minutes. Add the garlic and sauté until fragrant, about 30 seconds. Add the tomatoes, season with salt, and let stand for 1 minute without stirring, then continue cooking until a thick sauce forms, stirring frequently, about 15 minutes. Let cool slightly. Set a strainer over a heavy small saucepan. Strain the tomato mixture into the saucepan, pushing on the solids to extract all liquid. Stir in the vinegar and cook over medium heat, stirring frequently, until the mixture is the consistency of ketchup, about 25 minutes.

Peel the avocado. Place the flesh in a processor. Add the lemon juice, garlic, and a pinch of salt and purée until smooth. With the machine running, mix in the remaining 5 tablespoons olive oil. Transfer to a bowl. Stir the green onion into the aïoli.

Heat the vegetable oil in large heavy pot or deep fryer to 375°F (190°C).

Tear potatoes into bite-size pieces. Deep-fry potato pieces until golden brown (in batches; do not crowd), 5 to 7 minutes. Remove potatoes using slotted utensil and drain on paper towels. Serve immediately with ketchup and aïoli.

Cheese and Herb Phyllo Spirals with Shimon's Bizbaz

Master Chef Tom Franz pairs these delicate cheese-stuffed pastries with a fresh tomato salsa spiked with a spicy zhug condiment invented by his father-in-law, "who loves hot and spicy food and adds zhug to it and some more goodness and calls it *bizbaz*." The combination of the chilled, piquant tomato salsa and the crispy cheese-stuffed spirals is an inspired union of hot, cold, spicy, soft, chewy, and sweet.

BIZBAZ

6 large ripe tomatoes, quartered

¼ cup (60 ml) olive oil

3 tablespoons fresh lemon juice

1 tablespoon zhug (see facing page)

Pinch of brown sugar

Salt and freshly ground pepper

SPIRALS

½ cup (1 stick; 115 g) butter, melted

1 cup (75 g) crumbled feta cheese

1 cup (150 g) grated Gouda or Edam cheese

⅓ cup (50 g) pine nuts, toasted

⅓ cup (20 g) chopped fresh herbs, such as basil and oregano

Salt and freshly ground pepper

9 phyllo pastry sheets, defrosted and kept under a damp cloth

1 cup (240 ml) heavy cream

FOR BIZBAZ: Grate the tomato quarters with a hand-held grater until you reach the skin. Transfer the grated tomatoes to a bowl and discard the skins. Stir in the oil, lemon juice, zhug, and sugar. Season with salt and pepper. Cover and refrigerate until ready to use.

FOR SPIRALS: Preheat the oven to 350°F (175°C).

Brush a baking dish or casserole dish with some of the melted butter, reserving the rest for later. Place both cheeses, the pine nuts, and the herbs in a bowl and season with salt and pepper. Stir well to combine. Set the filling aside.

Layer 3 phyllo sheets on a work surface (cover remaining sheets with a damp towel to prevent drying). Brush the top layer with some of the remaining melted butter. Cut the layered phyllo into 4 equal pieces. Place 1 full tablespoon of filling at the bottom of the widest side of each piece. Spread filling evenly. Roll up the dough as you would a cigar and brush with some of the melted butter. Roll the "cigar" into a spiral shape. Place the spiral seam-side down in the prepared dish. Brush with some of the remaining melted butter. Repeat with the rest of the phyllo dough and filling to make 8 more spirals, for a total of 12. Pour the heavy cream over and around the spirals in the dish. Bake until the cream is absorbed and the pastries are golden, about 30 to 40 minutes.

Serve hot with bizbaz and extra zhug.

SHIMON HADARI'S ZHUG

This will probably make more than you will need, but there is always a use for this versatile Yemeni condiment.

2 fresh hot green chilies, stems removed

1 bunch cilantro, stems removed

1 head garlic, cloves removed and peeled

¼ teaspoon ground cumin

Salt and freshly ground pepper

Olive oil

Place the chilies, cilantro, garlic, and cumin in a food processor and pulse until a fine paste forms. Season with salt and pepper. Taste on a piece of bread and correct seasoning if necessary. Transfer to an airtight container and pour olive oil over the zhug to prevent it from spoiling. Cover and refrigerate until ready to use. Remember to make sure to cover the surface of the zhug with olive oil after each use.

Spinach and Feta Arayes

If you are lucky in life, you will find a dish that everyone in your family loves, and whenever you suggest making it, they will enthusiastically agree. This has become that recipe in my family. Asaf Doktor, chef and owner of Haachim, takes the Palestinian arayes, a grilled pita bread stuffed with chopped lamb, and reinvents it as vegetarian with spinach, onions, feta cheese, and za'atar. If you want this as a main course, double or triple the recipe and don't be alarmed about wasting anything; I discovered that popping them in the toaster is a great way to reheat them. Serve with the yogurt sauce on page 46.

¼ cup (60 ml) extra virgin olive oil

2 large red onions, halved and thinly sliced

3 large garlic cloves, thinly sliced

2 tablespoons chopped fresh oregano

2 teaspoons za'atar (page 91) or dried oregano

¾ pound (340 g) baby spinach leaves

½ cup (75 g) crumbled full-fat feta cheese

Salt and freshly ground pepper

4 pita breads

Additional olive oil

¼ cup (60 g) whole milk yogurt

Heat the olive oil in large heavy skillet over high heat. Add the onions and cook until they start to brown, stirring frequently, about 10 minutes. Reduce heat to medium and cook until onions soften, stirring occasionally, about 10 minutes. Add the garlic and sauté for 3 minutes. Stir in the fresh and dried oregano and za'atar and toss skillet several times. Add the spinach and sauté just until wilted, about 5 minutes. Season with salt and pepper; do not oversalt, as feta is salty. Transfer the filling to a strainer in the sink and let stand for 1 hour.

Transfer the filling to a bowl. Add the feta and mix well. Adjust seasoning with salt and pepper.

Cut each pita in half. Place an ample amount of the filling into each pita half. Lightly brush the outside of each pita with olive oil.

Heat a grill or panini press to medium or heat a large heavy skillet over medium heat. Add pitas to grill, press, or skillet and cook on each side until crispy and brown, 3 to 4 minutes per side. Cut each arayes in half. Serve with yogurt.

Fried Artichokes with Labneh

Asaf Doktor, the chef/owner of Haachim, which means "Brothers" in English (his are his business partners), told me that he could live on a desert island with just labneh, olive oil, and a piece of bread. I would add artichokes. And a frying pan. And fleur de sel. This is maybe the only instance in which I would consider eating a canned or frozen vegetable. The labneh, a thick Middle Eastern fresh cheese made from yogurt that has been strained to remove its whey, must be prepared a day in advance. I suggest doubling the recipe. The crispy golden thistles disappear quickly.

LABNEH

4 cups (960 g) whole milk yogurt, preferably 7 percent fat

1 lemon, halved

1 teaspoon salt

ARTICHOKES

24 canned or defrosted frozen baby artichoke quarters, drained and patted dry

3 cups (700 ml) vegetable oil (for deep-frying)

Salt

1/2 cup (20 g) chopped flat-leaf parsley leaves

4 medium garlic cloves, minced

FOR LABNEH: Spoon the yogurt into a large bowl. Squeeze the juice from each lemon half into yogurt. Add the salt and stir well to blend. Place a large strainer atop another large bowl. Line the strainer with cheesecloth or a clean, lightweight kitchen towel. Transfer yogurt to lined strainer. Place in the refrigerator and let stand overnight; the texture should be like whipped cream cheese. Transfer the labneh to a storage container and refrigerate until ready to use.

FOR ARTICHOKES: Preheat the oven to 200°F (93°C). Arrange two baking sheets on a work surface. Line one with paper towels.

Pour the oil into a heavy medium pot over medium heat and bring to 350°F (177°C). Add the artichokes to the oil (in batches; do not crowd) and fry until crispy and brown, 5 to 7 minutes. Using a slotted utensil, transfer artichokes from pot to paper-towel lined baking sheet, then transfer to regular baking sheet. Season with salt, then place in oven to keep warm if desired. Continue frying remaining artichokes.

TO SERVE: Divide labneh among 4 plates and spread well. Set 6 artichokes atop labneh on each plate. Garnish with the parsley and garlic. Serve immediately.

Orange and Black Olive Salad with Harissa

The surprising combination of oranges and salt-cured black olives is further enhanced in Master Chef Tom Franz's unique salad by dressing it with a rich harissa sauce. The sweet, salty, and spicy flavors fuse beautifully, and the optional addition of pieces of fresh salmon he added for the photograph bring it up a notch as a main-course ceviche-style salad.

HARISSA

7 ounces (200 g) dried sweet peppers

1 whole head garlic, cloves removed and peeled

1 bunch cilantro, leaves only

6 tablespoons fresh lemon juice

1 tablespoon salt

1 teaspoon ground cumin

1/2 teaspoon cayenne pepper

1 cup (240 ml) olive oil

SALAD

6 medium oranges, peeled and cut into cubes

5 tablespoons olive oil

1/4 cup (40 g) halved salt-cured pitted black olives

3 tablespoons fresh lemon juice

2 tablespoons chopped cilantro

1/2 teaspoon ground cumin

Salt

FOR HARISSA: Place dried peppers in a bowl. Cover with warm water and let stand for 1 hour. Drain. Cut ends off of peppers and discard. Transfer peppers to a food processor. Add garlic cloves and cilantro leaves and pulse to blend well. Add lemon juice, salt, cumin, and cayenne and pulse to blend to a paste. Transfer to an airtight glass container. Pour olive oil over the mixture and cover and refrigerate it until ready to use.

FOR SALAD: Combine the oranges, olive oil, black olives, lemon juice, cilantro, and cumin in a large bowl. Stir in 1 1/2 tablespoons harissa (reserve remainder for another use). Let stand at room temperature for 2 hours. Just before serving, add salt to taste if desired.

Claro's Sour Cream Ice Cream

In a dairy shop in the Carmel Market, I counted over fifteen metal containers of different varieties of soft white cheese in a refrigerated display case. It appeared to me as if they were selling clouds. This ice cream from Claro restaurant uses billowy sour cream and does not require any cooking; just blend, churn, and eat. Chef Ran Shmueli serves his oval nimbus with a fresh cherry crumble.

ICE CREAM

2 cups (475 ml) half and half

1¾ cups (450 g) sour cream

1½ cups (300 g) sugar

1 cup (240 ml) heavy cream, chilled

1 tablespoons fresh lemon or lime juice

1 tablespoon vanilla extract

Pinch of salt

CHERRY CRUMBLE

2 pounds (900 g) cherries, pitted

1 cup (100 g) sugar, divided

1 cup (60 g) all-purpose flour

1 cup (100 g) almond flour

½ cup (1 stick; 115 g) butter

ICE CREAM: Place all ingredients in a large metal bowl with an airtight lid and whisk until smooth and well combined. Cover and place in the freezer for 1 hour. Transfer the liquid to an ice cream maker and churn according to the manufacturer's instructions. After churning, transfer the ice cream to another airtight container and freeze for at least 2 hours before serving.

CHERRY CRUMBLE: Combine the cherries and ½ cup (50 g) of the sugar in a large bowl. Let stand at least 1 hour.

Preheat the oven to 325°F (160°C). Line a baking sheet with parchment paper. Combine the remaining ½ cup (50 g) sugar, both flours, and the butter in a food processor and pulse until the mixture comes together. Crumble the mixture onto the parchment-lined baking sheet and bake until fragrant and golden brown, about 25 minutes.

TO SERVE: Spoon some cherries and liquid into each of 8 shallow bowls. Top with ice cream, sprinkle with the crumble, and serve immediately.

THE NORTH

DRIVING NORTH ON THE YITZHAK RABIN HIGHWAY, I looked to my left at the deep blue Mediterranean Sea through a curtain of bright pink hollyhocks swaying gently in the breeze. Nancy and I were on our way to visit Erez Komarovsky at his home in Mattat, which lies on a mountaintop minutes from the Lebanese border. Throughout my travels, almost everyone asked me if I had been to see Erez yet. He looms large in the land of Israel, not unlike the Wizard of Oz, and has a sixth sense about flavor that evokes the same sensibility that Nancy possesses. In fact, both Nancy and Erez gained tremendous respect and acclaim as founders of successful bakeries. After spending time with Erez, I understood his popularity. He has an overflowing, generous spirit and makes everything he prepares look simple, beautiful, and tasty. He also understands the food revolution in Israel and explained it to me with the eloquence of a philosopher:

> It took time to develop a culinary language. For the first thirty years, only grandmothers and mothers cooked. All the restaurants cooked French food, but we didn't have the right ingredients and it was horrible. In the past 15 years, as Israel became richer, people had more money and could go to restaurants to eat. They traveled more and demanded more. Chefs wanted better vegetables, smaller artichokes, fresher meats, and different cheeses. Also, we were racist and everything that came from the Arabs, the East, Morocco was considered to be lowly—poor people's food, and now that has changed. Israel has this window of opportunity. Our knowledge is starting to be exported and Israeli cuisine is being taken outside of Israel. Are Jews smarter—better? Because we suffered so much we are trying to do better. We have a huge inferiority complex. We are thought of as chosen, but since so many of us were murdered, now we are trying to prove ourselves. Taste buds do not feel the burden of politics.

Erez was twenty-one years old when he finished his army service and went directly to Le Cordon Bleu in Paris because he was a romantic. "French, only French," was his mantra, but it was only after he lived in California that he understood what needed to be done in Israel. "We needed to develop a local culinary language that would consist of all the spices here," he told me.

The feast he served Nancy and me appeared in waves. A bread stuffed with cauliflower, another of whole grains, a challah with olives and fresh anchovies, a sacrilegious kugel made with bacon that had been baked for ten hours, and seared lamb with spices that he ground at the table before our eyes and flavored with the smoke from smoldering rose petals, which appeared and then vanished as if by magic. We wandered through his terraced gardens, which he called "a wild place of discovery," and talked about his decision to live so far out of the pale. He explained that he wanted to live in the mountains, but not too far from the sea. "The north is very similar to California, except here we come from Yemen, Poland, and Morocco." Erez buys his fresh fish from the Arab and Kurd coastal villages and believes that the fruits and vegetables are better in the mountains. There are very few restaurants nearby and he told me they all are awful. "The rural people cook at home and their traditions survive." He is not a fan of molecular cuisine—how could he be, with the kind of food he served us?—nor of The French Laundry, "where everything is cooked to perfection, then seared; our food is rough, burn it! This is Israel for me."

The views Erez commands from his outpost are sweeping and impressive, and standing on his terrace surveying the landscape made me realize how everything in the north is physically close yet very distinct in temperament. In the Western Galilee, there is Akko, an Arab town with long-standing Arab traditions, the sprawling port city of Haifa, and the villages of Clil and Yodfat, with their counterculture spirit. The Golan Heights is in the Upper Galilee, formerly a part of Syria but taken by Israel in the Six-Day War, and Nazareth is in the Lower Galilee. And strewn across this swath of northern Israel are some of the country's most delectable culinary treasures.

Miro, the sous chef at Savida, a small fish restaurant in the eighteenth-century Turkish Bazaar in Akko, told me that in Israel there is always a surprise and then another surprise. One person who appears not to be terribly overwrought by this state of affairs is Savida's unflappable chef and co-owner Dan Smulovitz. If the local fishermen don't have any acceptable fresh fish, he closes. If he runs out of fish, he closes. If customers ask too many questions, he tells them to leave and go to the nearby falafel place. He doesn't have a menu because he believes that without one, he has no contract with his guests and can remain loyal to his unwavering policy of serving only the freshest food possible. His bread is homemade, many of his greens are locally foraged, and his salad recipes change by the minute depending on the whims of Samira, one of the cooks in his compact kitchen, who was raised in a Bedouin camp, married at eight years old, and left her husband after he brought home a third wife.

Dan grew up on the nearby Ghetto Fighters Kibbutz, founded by rebels from the Warsaw Ghetto, and he admitted to me that survivors are not the easiest people to live with. I asked him whether, as a result of his childhood experiences, he sees the glass half empty or half full, and he replied, "I see the glass." Never overthinking or over-dressing his recipes, Dan collaborates with nature when he cooks. He only cooks with fire, never gas, because he believes the flavor is in the wood. The baked potatoes he serves with his grilled fish dishes are cooked in the coals of his grill. Dan's belief is that food should feed the soul, not the chef's ego.

The day I spent with him was festive and eventful, in part because that night, Yemen Blues, a band led by the singer-songwriter Ravid Kahalani, was playing at a club in Haifa and many of Dan's friends were going. While I was photographing Dan's fish and Samira's salads, a young man with piercing blue eyes obscured by a veil of haze intently watched me work. He thrust his cigarette toward me and murmured, "Hash, very sweet." I politely declined the offer but savored the exotic luster our exchange added to the atmosphere of the Turkish Bazaar. I accompanied Dan and his friends to Haifa to see the concert even though it had been sold out for weeks. Dan was confident that he could get me in, and he did.

Everyone I was with and others I met at the club told me I had no idea how miraculous it was that this Jewish singer attracted both an Arab and a Jewish audience and that the two typically distinct groups were intermingling in the same space. I couldn't easily distinguish the Jews from the Arabs. They were all young, good looking, and well dressed, singing along with the band and waving their arms in ecstasy. Someone shouted to me, "This is what should be on CNN, not the other bullshit." Ravid, the lead singer of Yemen Blues, spoke to the audience in English, flashed peace signs, and encouraged everyone to "be who you are, don't listen to propaganda or hate, and keep this spirit of being together alive." Ohad Orvitz, Dan's bald-headed co-owner at Savida, jumped up on the stage and danced with the singer, whose huge braided bun unraveled after his fifth song when he whipped his head around,

his long braids streaming down across his shoulders and back. They were a striking pair and the crowd roared in appreciation. Ravid's voice was high and deep and ragged, soulful and bluesy, and the music was loud. I was swept up by the emotions flying around in the small, dark space and wondered what my fellow passenger on the Italian train in 1984 would think about my unusual evening in Haifa. Over thirty years ago, my fleeting Israeli travel companion and I were the same age as the young people I was spending the evening with are now, and I was finally in Israel, deeply moved by my experiences. I wonder if my life would have taken a different path if I had made this journey in my twenties.

Because I was the designated driver for my new, younger friends, and because we were at the concert until past two in the morning, I spent the night at the Ghetto Fighters Kibbutz. This night marked my first stay on a kibbutz, and the next day, to celebrate, Dan took me to lunch at Sharabik, a restaurant in Rama, a small Arab village nearby. His friend Hazem Alzubi, a Jordanian ceramic artist, joined us. Hazem is married to a woman from Akko and commutes to his studio in Amman, Jordan, twice a week. Dan wanted Hazem and me to meet because he thought we had a lot in common, which turned out to be true. We both feel at home in foreign places, take pictures of trees and skies with our phones, listen to classical music when we drive, and were shaped by the places where we went to school in the 1970s, Berkeley and Baghdad. We have similar thoughts about our spirituality— he is Muslim and I am Jewish, neither one of us is observant—and we share a common language of art and philosophy. I travel and do the work I do because I am interested in learning about other ways of life and seeing the world from a different perspective from my own. When I am able to connect and find common ground with someone who has a different life experience in a vastly different geographic location, it enriches my understanding of a place and adds a deeper meaning to my work.

Sharabik is simplicity itself. Yaqub Hiat, a former social worker and Sharabik's chef and owner, told us that everything he does is simple. He told me that he tries, not always successfully, to respect the true flavors of the vegetable. Dan, Hazem, and I sat outside next to a parking lot at a table covered in plastic. We were served firm and flavorful small green olives; pickled cauliflower and turnips stained yellow with turmeric and pink from beet juice; pickled cucumbers; a lentil and onion salad; roasted eggplant with tahini; tomatoes in olive oil and fresh herbs; pita bread; hot sauce; and, finally, tea with a small bowl of tahini and carob sauce. While I savored each bite of what I was eating, I thought of how much Nancy would enjoy the fresh, spicy tastes here; so I reconfigured the itinerary I had planned for her visit a few weeks later so it would include Sharabik.

After lunch, Dan, Hazem, and I visited Ashkar Winery in Kfar Yasif. The owner is Nemi Ashkar, a tech executive for IBM whose family's land was confiscated by the new State of Israel in 1948. His stoic acceptance of the tragic irony that he buys his grapes from the current owners of the land that his family once owned surprised me. I told him that I write endless letters demanding justice when I feel I have been wronged, and that if something of that magnitude had happened to me without any possible remedy, I fear I would likely have lost my mind. I told him I admired the life he has lived in spite of the adversity he has faced.

Nemi produces about 13,000 bottles of wine per year in his cellar, which is under his house. Among them is a particularly good Cabernet Sauvignon with soft tannins and the pleasant flavor of dried figs. As we were leaving with the bottles of wine Nemi insisted we take with us, his wife, Amira, came home from baking Easter cookies—round, delicate, date-stuffed confections with an intricate

PREVIOUS OVERLEAF: VINEYARD VIEW LOOKING TOWARD THE SEA OF GALILEE.

design on the surface that perplexed me until I realized that I had seen the molds to make them at the Akko market a few days before. She urged us to taste one, and when I told her how delicious they were, she laughed and said, "Food is a refuge from our problems."

Amira's comment about needing to find a sanctuary from the turmoil of daily living in Israel, whether it is a cookie or a place, resonated with me when I visited Goats with the Wind in Yodfat, a goat cheese farm and restaurant a half hour's drive from Akko. Goats with the Wind feels as if it is in another world, a world I had no desire ever to leave. Approaching the entrance to the farm, I wound my way on a gravelly road through a landscape strewn with rocks and wild shrubs and dotted with olive trees. Off in the distance, clinging to a hillside, was Nazareth, whose native son Jesus has for millennia offered spiritual refuge to countless human souls.

Daliah Shpigel and Amnon Zaldestien are the masterminds behind this wedge of paradise. Their goats are strong and healthy, housed in a beautiful space surrounded by hand-wrought iron fences, hand-painted doors, and stone walls. Amnon manages the farm and makes the cheese, helped by volunteers and family members, and Daliah does the cooking.

I felt a bond with Daliah the minute I saw her. She bears an uncanny resemblance to my father's mother, a woman I never had the chance to meet. She is a true Lady of the Canyon, with cascading dark hair, strings of colored stones around her neck, layers of embroidered clothing on her sturdy frame, and tough, leather work boots on her feet. Her cooking appears effortless. She is pensive and focused, generous and warm, calm and spiritual. She chops and slices and tosses vegetables into the steaming terra-cotta tagines on her bright yellow stove in the kitchen, which remains open year-round to the sky, the hills, and the valley just below, where, I am told, contemporary archaeologists believe Jesus was born.

Everyone pops into Daliah's kitchen to say *boker tov* and *shalom*. Cats, peacocks, volunteers, packs of children, and her own children and grandchildren come by for a taste of something good. She feeds them slivers of goat cheese from a refrigerated set of drawers. She'll stop cooking long enough to hug a child while the tagines bubble and fizzle, and she'll take a break to sit on her terrace and drink tea in between feeding six to twelve family members and friends a day in addition to the guests in the restaurant.

Amnon, Daliah, a few volunteers, and I ate dinner sitting under the stars on cushions at a low table, with the lights of Nazareth glittering in the distance. Was the frisson I felt a chill from the night air, or the realization that I could be in Jerusalem, Damascus, Beirut, or Amman in roughly an hour?

Before we began eating, everyone sat silently. Amnon and Daliah closed their eyes for a few minutes, and when they opened them, Amnon asked Gal, a friend from Jerusalem, to say the prayer over the bread. The knives and forks were wrapped with a napkin and tied with a sprig of lavender. We ate Daliah's fragrant halloumi cheese flower—a dish of melted cheese simmering with tomatoes, garlic, chilies, and cilantro—big heads of lettuce drizzled with maple syrup, stinging nettle soup, bowls of quinoa, and a hearty selection of delicious goat cheeses with bread from the village. We drank homemade wine in small cups. During our meal, when Amnon told us this parable, I felt like I was in a scene from *Fiddler on the Roof,* listening to Tevye:

> One day, Mulia Nasreddin was sent by his wife to the butcher to buy some meat. "I'm sorry," said the butcher, "I have run out of meat. I do have liver, though, and a recipe that has been used in our family for generations. Anyone who tastes the dish praises it greatly." And so did the butcher provide Mulia Nasreddin with the unique and special recipe and with a slice of liver. And with that in hand, Mulia headed home. He soon grew tired, so he stopped to rest by the side of the road.

He sat down in the shade of a tree and set the liver by his side. While he was resting, a buzzard swooped in, snatched the liver, and flew away into the skies. "You foolish buzzard," Mulia shouted, "You might have the liver, but I have the recipe!"

I was intrigued by Amnon's choice of parables. Was he voicing his approval of my project, a collection of recipes and stories about Israel? Or was he trying to communicate something deeper—the idea that knowledge and understanding, symbolized by the recipe, is power and cannot be taken from us? Is the liver a metaphor for the material world—possessions and land—things that never last, regardless of how desperately we cling to them or how much blood is shed over them? Or was the story a red schmaltz herring, since every Israeli cook has told me that ingredients are what is most important?

Driving north from Goats with the Wind through the Golan Heights evoked strange and intense sensations in me. I was surrounded on all sides by enemy nations and couldn't help but wonder if one of their citizens might slip through the border and appear next to me while I was patiently waiting for the clouds to drift by so I could photograph the late-afternoon light that would bring the vineyard landscapes to life. What would I do if someone unsettling approached me? Jump in my car and drive away as fast as I could? But what if my "enemy" was there waiting for the light too? As one of my companions at the concert in Haifa suggested, the media has set us up to fear each other. When the afternoon light began to fade, I drove along the unfamiliar roads and became aware of the increasingly numerous sparkling pinpoints of light on the distant hills. These were the lights in the homes of the "enemies." The car radio was tuned to the classical station that plays show tunes in the evenings, and in a surreal moment, Eliza Doolittle was telling me that all she wanted was a room somewhere. I wondered what the people whose lights I could see in the distance were making for dinner in their kitchens, what their kitchens looked like, what their conversations were about, and if they laughed and poured themselves glasses of Arak to unwind from their days. Is what they eat as important to them and their families as it is to us?

The eastern sky was a deep black when I arrived at Pausa, the inn owned by Einat and Avigdor Rothem, and the vineyards on the knoll right in front of the entrance were bathed in the last rays of golden sunlight from the west. The early evening air was fresh and fragrant from the recent rains. I appreciated this kind of welcome.

Avigdor Rothem is a burly man with a mischievous grin and a strange accent when speaking English, different from the accent most Israelis have. When I asked him about it, he explained that he was born in Moscow and moved to Israel with his family when he was nine. As a child in the underground Russian Zionist movement, he had never had friends his own age. Now, as an adult, he craves human contact. "For me," he explained, "Facebook is real. I have 2,000 friends and ninety percent of them are real friends. I'm not so much a family person. I'm a friend person." At the age of fourteen, Avigdor went to military school, where he started cooking Chinese and Japanese recipes from cookbooks given to him as gifts. He still loves to feed people. "The way I impress myself is not playing music, not painting; this is my art, my most human deep communication," he told me.

Everything grown in Pausa's one-acre garden is served to the guests. Avigdor's recipes are inspired by what he has on hand—even the soap in my bedroom was made from their lavender. He makes his own prosciutto, sauerkraut, and grappa. "For 300 years farmers prepared things from their fruits and vegetables," he explains. "I like life as it was." He and Einat dry and marinate fruits and cook and freeze tomatoes, and Avigdor's mother makes a kumquat marmalade that flung me into a deep reverie when I tasted it the next morning.

Like a tale straight out of a Russian novel, Avigdor related to me that he said to Einat at their first meeting, "You don't know it yet, but you are going to be my wife." She was twenty years old at the time and I could easily understand why he felt that way. Einat has long, dark hair parted in the middle and a radiant warmth that affects everyone around her. She grew up on a nearby kibbutz, "a place where war is about to come,"she fears, yet she is staunchly optimistic, believing in the possibility of good relations with neighbors because "we can't live any other way." I asked her what she loves about where she lives. I silently wondered why, if she was able to choose to live and raise her own children in a place free of the constant threat she described, she would choose to raise them in this volatile part of the country. She answered succinctly, "Green, quiet, and good people." As a parent raising children in an environment like the Upper Galilee, Einat believes it is important to be able to trust the people around her. In addition to the text messages everyone in the village receives from the head of security if there is an incident, they rely on each other. If she is away from home and something happens, she can trust her neighbors to be calm and lead her daughters to a safe location and take care of them. Food is central to this trust net. Neighbors grow things and trade them. The practice of being trusting and trusted is in the exchange of food. "You have it, you need it, and it's tasty, " Einat explains. Her new neighbor, an eighty-two-year-old Moroccan woman, recently needed help with something, and Einat assisted her. As an offer of thanks, the neighbor asked Einat if she'd like some grapefruits, because her tree is big and no one eats them. Einat waited a few days, went over and picked grapefruits, and when she finished, she asked the woman if she would like some lemons. The woman wanted to know if there were any small ones. Einat brought her a bag of small lemons, and a few weeks later, the woman brought Einat a jar of conserved lemons. This is what she likes most about where she lives: the sharing.

It rained intermittently for the three days I was at Pausa and I explored the misty, gray environs, hoping I would have the good fortune to be in a beautiful spot when the sun emerged. Ronit Vered had kindled my imagination when she told me about a bakery near the Syrian border, and the sommelier Aviram Katz had urged me to visit Pelter, a winery with varietals named after clouds and goat cheeses whose packaging bears the logo of a butterfly, symbolizing freedom.

Tal Pelter, cloud watcher, winemaker, and proprietor of Pelter Winery, is tall and lanky, with close-cropped salt-and-pepper hair and a generous smile. When I met him at his winery, he was in a rush to get home. His wife, Inbal, who was tending to their five children, needed to milk the goats. He quickly told me that he prefers low population density and appreciates the Golan for its wide-open spaces, which are unusual in Israel. Because of the minefields left behind by the Syrians, Tal explains, the Golan is "a sanctuary for animals, trees . . . all nature." Fiercely loyal to his honest, Israeli nature, when I told him I live in the Napa Valley, in California, he quickly and definitively stated that he doesn't care too much for the wines there.

I tasted Matar, a well-oaked kosher Chardonnay, whose name, according to Tal, means, "rain but more poetic—more like drizzle." I loved the wine's aggressive tangy acidity. It was the perfect companion to Inbal's aged tomme. The Pelter Unoaked Chardonnay was bright, lean, and minerally, and the 2014 Gewürztraminer had an elegant floral bouquet. The area where he grows Cabernet Sauvignon, Sauvignon Blanc, and Pinot Noir is cool, dry, volcanic, and 3,200 to 4,500 feet above sea level. There is plenty of sunlight ensuring scalding hot days, and the high altitude cools the fruit at night, bringing about a slow ripening process and a complex range of flavors.

The next morning, before traveling south to Magdalena restaurant on the Sea of Galilee, I visited the bakery Ronit had told me about in the Druze village Majdal Shams. It lies in the foothills of Mt.

Hermon, and as I ascended, the fog deepened and I could barely see a foot ahead of me. Never one to turn my back on a potentially uncomfortable situation that might reveal something I have never experienced before, I soldiered on with these directions: "When you arrive in the town, go through the first roundabout and when you reach the second roundabout, turn right at the statue of Sultan Al-Atrash [who led the Druze revolt against French colonialism in the early twentieth century] and the bakery will be on your right. There is no sign, so you might have to ask." Even if I could see what was around me, these directions would be challenging, especially because both roundabouts had statues as their key décor elements and there was no address to put into WAZE.

After a few circles through the town, I felt like I was ready for a round of pin the tail on the donkey, except there was no need for a blindfold. I stopped and asked a gas station attendant for help. When he got over the fact that a live person from California was standing before him, he clarified the route and I was parked in front of the bakery within ninety seconds.

The bakery was dingy but the aroma was heavenly. When I turned and looked in the corner, I melted at the sight of a Druze woman, wrapped in scarves, presiding over the saj, a black iron concave oven. Did Vermeer come here for inspiration for *The Kitchen Maid*? She was baking manakish, a flatbread covered either with sweet red peppers or za'atar. The owner, Samar Abu Jabal, had given me permission to photograph only the baker's hands, but when I showed her an image that included the woman's shrouded head but did not reveal her face, she approved and gave me a bag of manakish for the road and forced me to sit down and eat a slice of steaming hot fatayer, a bread stuffed with grated potatoes. Eating a double starch meal is my forte and I could easily have finished off the whole pie, which was about eighteen inches across, but lunch at Magdalena beckoned. When I emerged from the time-warped bakery, the fog had disappeared and I was surprised to see more BMWs in this town than in the whole of Israel. As I drove off, I admired the Shouting Hill, infamous in the pre–cell phone era because Druze families separated by the Israeli-Syrian conflict would communicate with megaphones from opposite sides of the border. I chuckled to myself thinking that for some families, this might be considered an ideal situation.

The travel distances are relatively short in Israel, and I was able to leave the ethereal Majdal Shams and arrive at a table with a view of the Sea of Galilee at Magdalena just in time for lunch. Joseph Hanna, the chef-owner, grew up in the kitchen of his parents' restaurant in Akko, where his mother cooked elaborate meals for large weddings. He is Christian Arab and studied architecture in Rameh. He worked as an architect for six years, until he became fed up with the narrow-minded mentality of his clients, who did not respect his training or his knowledge. Earning a living was a challenge, so he made the decision to return to the kitchen.

He opened two other restaurants before deciding to realize a long-harbored dream to create what the Israelis call a "chef restaurant." Joseph's vision was to remake Arab cuisine. Magdalena's interior is sleek and modern, with beautifully crafted ceramics by local artists. Rich, thick bowls, oversized plates, and delicate leaves made from clay fill the glass display cases at the entrance, which is located above a bustling supermarket with views of the Sea of Galilee, the largest freshwater lake in Israel and the lowest on the planet. I know of no other place to savor a delicious fattoush salad, fried cauliflower with green tahini and chili, and a vegetarian kubbeh while gazing at the body of water that was the scene of so many unique events in human history.

AMNON ZALDESTIEN AND DALIAH SHPIGEL, OWNERS OF GOATS WITH THE WIND IN YODFAT.

Siniya of Sea Bass

Most of the Siniya recipes I encountered in Israel were made with meat, so when Chef Alaa Muse served me this version with fish in his restaurant El Marsa in Akko, I was interested in tasting something different. The creamy tahini sauce is a rich and delicious accompaniment to the firm, fresh fish, and this recipe has become one of my favorites.

1½ cups (350 ml) water

½ cup (120 g) raw tahini

3 tablespoons fresh lemon juice

2 garlic cloves, minced

Salt and freshly ground white
 pepper

6 tablespoons olive oil, divided

8 cauliflower florets

1 pound 5 ounces (600 grams)
 skin-on sea bass fillet, cut into
 4 pieces

1 large russet potato, baked and
 quartered (do not peel)

Fresh dill sprigs

2 tablespoons toasted pine nuts

½ teaspoon ground sumac

Preheat oven to 400°F (200°C). Combine the water, tahini, lemon juice, and garlic in a small bowl and stir until smooth. Season with salt and pepper. Set the sauce aside until ready to use.

Heat 3 tablespoons of the olive oil in a heavy small skillet over medium heat. Add the cauliflower florets and sauté until golden brown, stirring occasionally so they color evenly on all sides.

Heat a heavy medium ovenproof skillet over medium-high heat. Coat the fish fillets with the remaining 3 tablespoons olive oil and season with salt and pepper. Place fillets in the heated skillet and cook for 3 minutes. Turn and cook 1 minute on the second side. Add cauliflower and potato to the skillet and pour tahini sauce over it. Transfer to the oven and bake until fish is cooked through, about 3 minutes. Garnish with dill, pine nuts, and sumac and serve immediately.

Spiced Lamb Kabobs

MAKES 14 KABOBS

I photographed these kabobs at a party I attended in Nazareth honoring the artisan cooks and chefs whom journalist Ronit Vered had written about in her column in the newspaper *Haaretz*. The aroma of the meat cooking on the flames mingled with the perfume of the burning cinnamon stick intoxicated me. They were prepared by Duhul Safdi, the chef and owner of Diana restaurant in Nazareth, where Nancy and I later tasted a memorable whole roasted eggplant that inspired her recipe on page 96. Duhul promised to send me his recipes, but after endless reminders, he never did. I couldn't let go of the kabobs, though, especially because I loved the photograph, and at lunch with Erez Komarovsky in Tel Aviv, I shared my frustration about Duhul's kabobs. Erez laughed and said Duhul used to work for him, and then dictated the recipe to me from memory.

1 tablespoon black peppercorns

1 teaspoon allspice berries

5 cardamom pods

1/2 teaspoon ground cinnamon

1/4 teaspoon ground nutmeg

2 pounds (1 kg) ground lamb, half lean and half fatty

2 medium onions, finely chopped

1/2 cup (20 g) finely chopped parsley

1/2 cup (20 g) chopped mint leaves

1/2 cup (70 g) toasted pine nuts

1 tablespoon salt

14 (5-inch; 13 cm) cinnamon sticks

Place the peppercorns, allspice, and cardamom in a mortar and grind them with a pestle. Place the spice mixture in a bowl and toss with the ground cinnamon and nutmeg.

Preheat a grill, plancha, or cast-iron skillet.

Place the lamb in a large bowl. Add the onions, parsley, mint, pine nuts, and salt. Add at least 1 tablespoon of the spice blend (reserve the remainder for another use), or add more or all if you like your meat well spiced. Using clean hands, knead the meat mixture until well combined. Mold about 3 ounces (85 g) of meat around each cinnamon stick, leaving about 3 inches of the stick exposed to become a handle. Grill kabobs on the grill (do not crowd) with a little bit of the cinnamon stick on each, turning to cook all sides, until cooked through, about 10 minutes (or less if you prefer your lamb a bit pink). Serve immediately.

Aromatic Stuffed Grape Leaves

In the early spring, I foraged large Jerusalem sage leaves with Daliah Shpigel at her farm Goats with the Wind in Yodfat. We stuffed them with this fragrant mixture of nuts, fresh herbs, and rice, and she taught me how to roll them tightly. If you cannot find Jerusalem sage, Daliah recommends using fresh grape leaves or Swiss chard.

5 tablespoons olive oil, divided

1 medium onion, finely chopped

5 garlic cloves, minced

1 medium-size ripe tomato, finely chopped

1 cup medium-grain rice, rinsed well

1½ cups (350 ml) water

½ bunch mint, finely chopped (about 1 cup, 40 g)

½ bunch cilantro, finely chopped (about 1 cup, 40 g)

½ bunch dill, finely chopped (about ½ cup, 20 g)

2 tablespoons pine nuts, toasted

2 tablespoons shelled raw pistachios, toasted and coarsely chopped

Salt and freshly ground pepper

32 grape leaves, blanched if fresh

1 large ripe red tomato

¼ cup (60 ml) water

Heat 2 tablespoons of the oil in a heavy medium skillet over medium heat. Add the onion and garlic and sauté until golden brown, about 10 minutes. Add the chopped tomato and sauté until slightly thickened, about 5 minutes. Stir in the rice and 1½ cups (350 ml) water and bring to a boil. Reduce the heat, cover, and simmer until the rice is tender and no liquid remains, about 15 minutes. Stir in all of the chopped herbs and both nuts. Season filling generously with salt and pepper. Let cool.

Preheat the oven to 300°F (150°C). Rub 1 tablespoon of the olive oil on a baking sheet. Set a grape leaf on your work surface with the veins facing up. Mound 1 scant tablespoon filling on the bottom of the leaf, leaving a border. Fold in the sides of the leaf, and then roll the leaf up over the filling to make a cylinder. Set the grape leaf seam-side down on the prepared baking sheet. Repeat with the remaining grape leaves and filling, packing bundles close together on the baking sheet.

Grate the large tomato into a bowl. Stir in ¼ cup (60 ml) water and the remaining 2 tablespoons oil. Pour the tomato mixture over the stuffed grape leaves. Cover baking sheet with foil. Bake for 45 minutes. Serve grape leaves warm, at room temperature, or chilled.

OVERLEAF: JEWISH KIBBUTZNIK ADAM ZIV AND MUSLIM ARAB ALAA SAWITAT, CO-OWNERS OF BOUZA ICE CREAM PARLOR IN TARSHIHA.

Lamb Komarovsky

"Smoke is the best flavor I know," confides Erez Komarovsky as he conjures up these seared lamb loin fillets at the table. He serves the lamb tataki style, seared on the outside and very rare on the inside. If you cannot find fillets, use lamb rib chops, two or three per person, and cook them in the same way. In the winter, Erez serves an accompanying salad made with fresh za'atar leaves, and in the summer, with "gentle" oregano leaves. If you can't find either, use field greens mixed with fresh oregano.

1 teaspoon ground turmeric

1/2 teaspoon ground mace

1 jalapeño, deveined and seeded if desired

1 cup (240 ml) fresh organic rose petals or 8 dried rosebuds

7 tablespoons olive oil, divided

2 lamb loin fillets

Salt and freshly ground pepper

1 cup (55 g) microgreens or mixed field greens

1/2 cup (20 g) fresh oregano leaves

1 1/2 cups (200 g) thinly sliced sweet onion

2 tablespoons ground sumac

1 lemon, halved

Combine the turmeric, mace, jalapeño, and rose petals using a mortar and pestle or a mini food processor. Add 3 tablespoons of the olive oil and pound or mix to a paste. Rub the paste on the lamb. Season with salt and pepper.

Heat a grill, plancha, or cast-iron skillet over medium-high heat until very hot. Place lamb on the hot surface and cook until seared on the outside but still very rare inside, 2 to 3 minutes per side. Transfer meat to a cutting board and let stand while making the salad.

Combine the greens, oregano, onion, and sumac in bowl. Drizzle with the remaining 4 tablespoons olive oil. Squeeze the lemon over the salad. Season with salt and pepper.

Divide salad among 4 plates. Cut the lamb into slices, divide them among the plates, and set atop the salad. Serve immediately.

Salmon Roll with Pickled Fennel

With his prophetic appearance, I expected Uri Jeremias to utter the absolute truths we were all waiting to hear, but it turned out he is just a great cook, which might be the only truth that matters. He is one of the pioneers of modern Israeli cuisine and his restaurant Uri Buri in Akko is a gastronomic Mecca.

PICKLED FENNEL

½ cup (120 ml) rice wine vinegar

½ cup (100 g) sugar

1 tablespoon ouzo or Arak

2 fennel bulbs, trimmed and chopped

SALMON

½ cup (120 ml) soy sauce

¼ cup (60 ml) rice wine vinegar

½ cup (120 ml) water

3 tablespoons fresh orange juice

2 tablespoons sugar

1½ tablespoons grated orange peel

1 tablespoon fresh lemon juice

1 tablespoon grated lemon peel

½ teaspoon sesame oil

½ teaspoon ground ginger

Pinch of coriander seeds

2 (4-ounce; 113 g) salmon fillets

2 sheets nori seaweed

¼ cup (30 g) all-purpose flour

2 eggs

¼ cup (30 g) panko

SAUCE

1 cup (240 ml) soy sauce

2 tablespoons sugar

1 tablespoon ouzo or Arak

¼ cup (60 ml) cold water

1 tablespoon cornstarch

ASSEMBLY

Vegetable or canola oil

FOR FENNEL: Place the vinegar in a bowl. Add the sugar and stir to dissolve. Stir in the ouzo. Add the fennel and stir well. Cover and refrigerate for at least 2 days before using. After draining, reserve 1 cup of the pickling liquid for the sauce.

FOR SALMON: Combine the first 11 ingredients in a baking dish. Add the salmon and marinate for 10 minutes. Remove salmon from the marinade; reserve marinade for later use.

Place the seaweed sheets on a work surface. Brush both sides with salmon marinade. Place a salmon fillet atop each piece of seaweed and roll up tightly. Place the flour in a shallow bowl. Break the eggs into another shallow bowl and beat to blend. Place the panko in a third shallow bowl. Dredge the seaweed-wrapped salmon in flour, shaking off any excess, then dip it in the egg, allowing the excess to drip back into the bowl. Dredge in panko. Set the wrapped and coated salmon on a plate and refrigerate for at least 2 hours before frying.

FOR SAUCE: Combine the first 3 ingredients in a small heavy saucepan. Stir in 1 cup (240 ml) of the fennel pickling liquid and bring to a boil. Meanwhile, place the cold water in a small bowl. Add the cornstarch and stir to blend. Add the mixture to saucepan and stir until silky. Reduce heat and keep warm.

TO ASSEMBLE: Heat the oil in a deep fryer or large heavy pot to 350°F (175°C). Fry the salmon until it is cooked through and golden brown on both sides. Remove from oil. Let cool slightly. Cut salmon into slices and arrange on a serving platter. Drizzle with sauce. Garnish with pickled fennel and serve.

FACING, TOP: URI JEREMIAS, CHEF AND OWNER OF URI BURI IN AKKO.

Sea Bass with Pickled Chilies, Yellow Rice, and Coconut-Apple Sauce

4 SERVINGS

By preparing the pickled chilies five days in advance, this recipe is less daunting than it might seem, and the payoff is worth it. Uri Jeremias of Uri Buri in Akko is an autodidactic chef who abhors trends, relies on his intuition, and tries to create interesting juxtapositions of flavor and texture. I think he has exceeded his own expectations here, quickly cooking the freshest fish in a hot cauldron, layering it with a spicy coconut milk sauce and apples, and then serving it over a delicate and fragrant jasmine rice.

PICKLED CHILIES

4 hot red finger peppers

4 small jalapeños

4 garlic cloves

1/2 lemon, seeded

3 tablespoons fresh lemon juice

3 tablespoons pickled green mango*

3 tablespoons rice wine vinegar

2 tablespoons sunflower oil

1 teaspoon salt

1 teaspoon finely chopped peeled fresh ginger

1/2 teaspoon ground turmeric

YELLOW RICE

2 tablespoons sunflower oil

1 cup (190 g) jasmine rice

1 1/2 (350 ml) cups water

1 rosemary sprig

1/2 teaspoon ground turmeric

Salt and freshly ground pepper

FISH

2 cups (475 ml) coconut milk

1 tablespoon sunflower oil

4 large fillets of sea bass, halibut, or cod

Salt and freshly ground pepper

2 medium-size tart green apples, cored, quartered, and cut into chunks

FOR PICKLED CHILIES: Place all ingredients in a food processor and grind to a rough paste. Transfer to a nonreactive bowl. Cover and refrigerate for at least 5 days.

FOR RICE: Heat the oil in a medium-size heavy pot over medium heat. Add the rice and stir until it is white. Meanwhile, combine the water, rosemary, and turmeric in a small heavy pot and bring to a boil. Stir the water into the rice, cover, and return to a boil. Reduce heat and simmer gently until the water is absorbed, about 15 minutes. Remove from heat and let stand for 15 minutes. Fluff with a fork. Season with salt and pepper.

FOR FISH: Meanwhile, pour the coconut milk into a bowl. Stir in 2 tablespoons of the pickled chilies (reserve the remainder for another use.) Brush the inside of a cast-iron skillet with the oil and heat over medium heat. Season the fish with salt and pepper. Add fish to the skillet and cook for 2 minutes per side. Pour coconut milk over the fish. Add the apples. Cover and cook for 4 minutes. Using a slotted utensil, transfer the fish to four plates. Stir sauce into the rice. Spoon rice alongside the fish and serve.

* Pickled green mango, known in Israel as *amba*, is available in specialty stores and by mail order. It is also available in Hispanic markets; one brand is La Toña, Mango Verde.

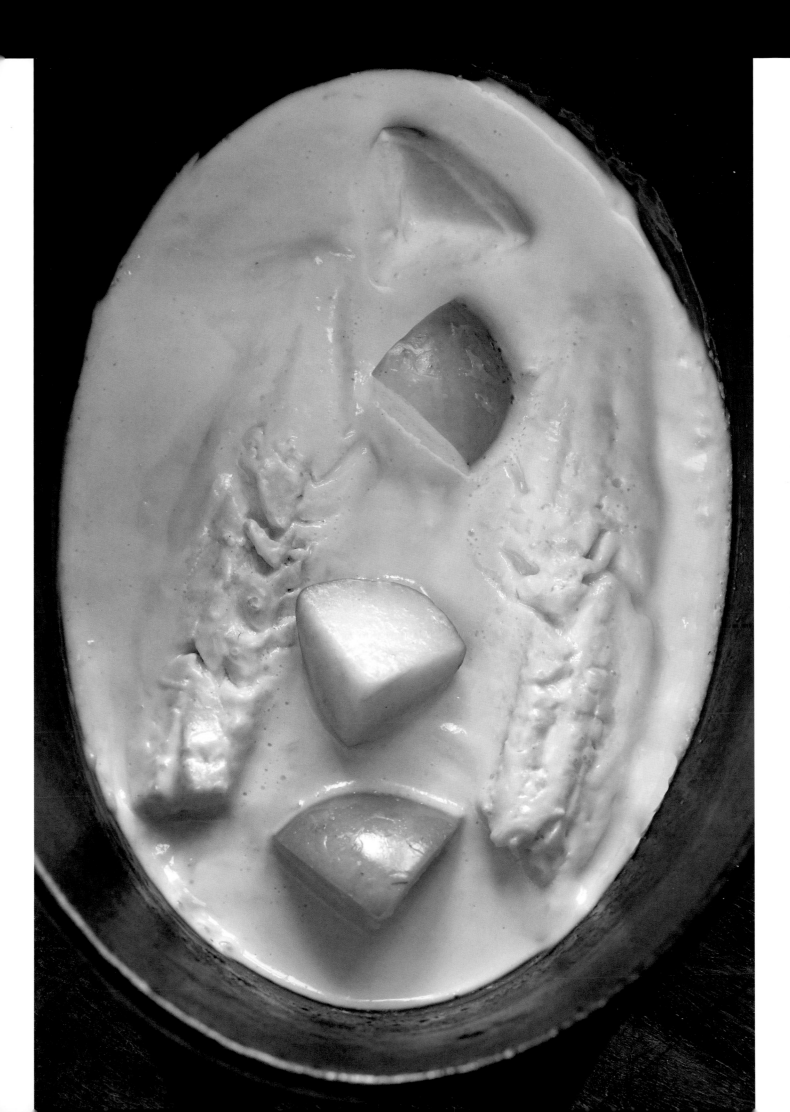

Carrot, Cilantro, and Preserved Lemon Salad with Sweet Chili Dressing

4 SERVINGS

I asked Amos Ostraich of Jacko in Haifa when he had decided to become a chef, and he threw up his arms in a global gesture and announced, "I am cook. Chefs you have only in France." Yet if a salad this fresh and simple were placed before me at Le Grand Véfour in Paris, I would not be disappointed.

½ cup (120 ml) plus 1 tablespoon extra virgin olive oil

½ cup (120 ml) sweet chili paste

¼ cup (60 ml) fresh lemon juice

1 teaspoon sugar

1 teaspoon salt

1 teaspoon ground cumin

¼ teaspoon cayenne pepper

1 pound (450 g) carrots, peeled and julienned

1 bunch cilantro, roughly chopped

1 whole preserved lemon, finely chopped (page 101)

Whisk the first 7 ingredients in a bowl to make the dressing. Toss the carrots, cilantro, and lemon in a salad bowl. Pour dressing over the salad; toss well and serve.

Cabbage Salad with Sesame and Soy Sauce

8 FIRST-COURSE OR SIDE-DISH SERVINGS

The ten salads in this photograph were simultaneously placed before me when I sat down to eat at Jacko in Haifa. The sesame and soy flavors of this one surprised me. I hadn't expected Asian seasonings in a seafood restaurant in Israel, but I loved every crunchy bite. For a colorful variation, use both green cabbage and red cabbage.

½ cup (120 ml) red wine vinegar

½ cup (120 ml) soy sauce

½ cup (120 ml) sesame oil

½ cup (100 g) sugar

1 medium green cabbage, cored and thinly sliced

¼ cup (40 g) toasted or roasted sesame seeds

Place the first 4 ingredients in a blender and blend well. Toss the cabbage and sesame seeds in a salad bowl. Pour the sauce over everything; toss well and serve.

Sweet and Sharp Beet Salad

I had never thought of eating raw beets before I tasted this crunchy and sweet salad while dining under the Ottoman arches of the Turkish Bazaar at Savida restaurant in Akko, and after I did, I appreciated this versatile vegetable even more than I had before.

4 medium beets, peeled and cut into cubes

1 small red onion, finely chopped

1 tablespoon thyme leaves

2 tablespoons apple cider vinegar

2 tablespoons pomegranate molasses

1 tablespoon silan (date syrup) or honey

1/4 cup (60 ml) extra virgin olive oil

Salt and freshly ground pepper

2 green onions, green part only, chopped

Place the beet cubes in a serving bowl. Add the onion and thyme.

Place the vinegar, pomegranate molasses, and silan in a small bowl and whisk well. Whisk in the oil in a steady stream. Season the dressing with salt and pepper. Add dressing to taste to the salad (you might have leftover dressing) and toss well. Adjust the seasoning with additional salt and pepper. Garnish with green onion tops and serve.

RECIPE PICTURED ON PAGE 93, MIDDLE RIGHT.

Yogurt, Walnut, and Horseradish Dip

This is a real workhorse dipping sauce dreamed up by the Savida team in Akko. Try it with roasted vegetables, on a falafel, with pita chips, or slathered over a baked potato.

1 cup (250 g) whole milk yogurt

1/2 cup (60 g) chopped toasted walnuts

1 tablespoon grated fresh horseradish

1 teaspoon fresh lemon juice

Salt and freshly ground pepper

Blend the yogurt, walnuts, horseradish, and lemon juice in a serving bowl. Season with salt and pepper and serve.

RECIPE PICTURED ON PAGE 92, BOTTOM LEFT.

Halloumi Cheese Flower

This soft, fresh cheese simmering with plump red tomatoes and seasoned with garlic, chili, and cilantro is presented in the shape of a savory flower blossom. A single flower will only make you crave a bouquet. Serve with warm pita.

3 tablespoons olive oil

1 medium-size ripe red tomato, halved and thinly sliced

3 to 4 ounces (85 to 110 g) halloumi or mozzarella cheese, thinly sliced

Salt and freshly ground pepper

3 large garlic cloves, thinly sliced

1 small fresh green chili, thinly sliced

10 cilantro sprigs

Heat oil in a heavy 8-inch (20 cm) skillet over medium heat. Arrange the tomato slices in a skillet in the shape of a circle. Top tomato slices with the cheese slices. Sprinkle with salt and pepper. Arrange the garlic and chili slices atop the cheese. Bunch the cilantro sprigs in the center of the skillet. Continue cooking until cheese is soft but not totally melted. Serve immediately.

Parsley and Mint Pesto

MAKES ABOUT 2 CUPS (450 GRAMS)

Everyone I know swears by a different pesto recipe, and I am always eager to taste a new version. Hagit Lidror served me this one in her kitchen in Clil, a place she describes as "out of the system," which also describes this surprising concoction. Your imagination is the only limiting factor on how to use it. Try it on potatoes, pizza, a wedge of cheese, or directly into the mouth by the spoonful.

4 cups (160 g) firmly packed flat-leaf parsley leaves

¾ cup (30 g) mint leaves

½ cup (70 g) raw unsalted sunflower seeds

⅓ cup (45 g) raw pine nuts

2 thin lemon slices, peel on

2 large garlic cloves, peeled

2 tablespoons fresh lemon juice

½ cup (120 ml) plus 2 tablespoons extra virgin olive oil

Salt and freshly ground pepper

Combine the first 7 ingredients in a food processor. Pulse until the mixture is finely chopped; do not overmix. With the machine running, blend in the olive oil. Season with salt and pepper.

Grilled Zucchini Salad

6 TO 8 SERVINGS

Here is another simple and delicious salad from Savida in Akko to add to the list of inventive Israeli salads. Serve it as an appetizer with as many other salads as you can fit on your table.

8 medium zucchini

3 medium garlic cloves, minced

1 tablespoon dried mint, crumbled

¼ cup (60 ml) fresh lemon juice

¼ cup (60 ml) extra virgin olive oil

Salt and freshly ground pepper

⅓ cup (40 g) chopped roasted pistachio nuts

Preheat a grill or broiler.

Grill or broil the whole zucchinis, turning frequently, until they are slightly charred on the outside. Let cool slightly, then cut into rounds. Place the zucchini rounds in a serving bowl. Toss with garlic and mint. Dress with lemon juice and olive oil. Season with salt and pepper. Garnish with nuts.

OVERLEAF: THE SALADS AT SAVIDA IN AKKO.
RECIPE PICTURED BOTTOM RIGHT.

Olive, Caper, and Herb Spread

MAKES ABOUT 2 1/2 CUPS (400 GRAMS)

This flavorful spread, created by Hagit Lidror, can hold its own on a thick slice of grilled bread rubbed with garlic and doused with olive oil, or it can be tossed with bucatini pasta for a simple and delicious supper.

2 cups (360 g) pitted Mediterranean green olives
2 tablespoons drained capers
1 tablespoon fresh lemon juice
1/4 medium lemon, seeded
1 tablespoon fresh oregano or thyme leaves
1/2 cup (120 ml) extra virgin olive oil
Freshly ground pepper

Combine the olives, capers, lemon juice, 1/4 lemon, and oregano in a food processor and pulse to coarsely chop. With the machine running, add the oil and pulse to blend. Season with pepper. Transfer to a bowl and serve. (If storing, drizzle a thin layer of olive oil over the top of the spread, cover and refrigerate.)

Fresh Za'atar Spread

MAKES ABOUT 1 1/2 CUPS (200 GRAMS)

Hagit Lidror told me that when the Israelites marked their door posts with lamb's blood so the angel of death would pass over them, God instructed them to use a bunch of hyssop as a paintbrush (Exodus 12:22). This was probably because hyssop was sturdy and could withstand the brushing, but it also likely signified that God was marking His people as "pure" and not targets of the judgment that He was about to mete out to the Egyptians. Please don't let this dour tale spoil your appetite. This spread is excellent on Hagit's Magic Kesem Crackers (page 124), as a dip for fresh vegetables, or as the highlight of a sandwich.

2 cups (80 g) fresh hyssop leaves (if unavailable, use Mexican oregano leaves)
1/2 cup (120 ml) extra virgin olive oil
1 tablespoon fresh lemon juice
1/4 teaspoon ground sumac
1/4 teaspoon ground cumin
Salt and freshly ground pepper

Combine the first 5 ingredients in a food processor. Pulse to blend well, but do not overmix. Season with salt and pepper. If you are not serving the spread immediately, place it in a bowl and seal it with a layer of olive oil, then cover and refrigerate.

Zahara

If I ruled the world, my first order of business would be to change the name of The Promised Land to The Land of Cauliflower. The Israelis love this cruciferous vegetable as much as I do and use it in countless creative ways. Chef Joseph Hanna elevates his presentation of golden fried cauliflower to a work of art with his accompanying green tahini sauce and garnishes of fresh herbs, radishes, and thinly sliced red hot peppers.

1 cup (40 g) chopped parsley

2 cups (480 g) tahini

1 cup (240 ml) water

1/2 cup (120 ml) fresh lemon juice

Salt and freshly ground pepper

Vegetable or canola oil (for deep-frying)

1 large cauliflower, trimmed and quartered

All-purpose flour

Place the parsley in a food processor and pulse it into a purée. Add the tahini, water, and lemon juice and process until the sauce is smooth and uniformly green. Season to taste with salt and pepper.

Heat the oil to 375°F (190°C) in a deep fryer or large heavy pot. Meanwhile, steam or parboil the cauliflower quarters until they are half-cooked.

Place the flour in a large shallow bowl and season with salt and pepper. Dredge cauliflower quarters in the flour, shaking off excess. Place cauliflower quarters in the oil and deep-fry until cooked through and golden brown, about 2 minutes. Remove from the oil and drain on paper towels. Spoon the sauce around the cauliflower. Refrigerate and save any leftover sauce for another use.

Nancy's Whole Roasted Eggplant with Hummus Tahini, Za'atar, and Zhug

Diana restaurant in Nazareth was one of the few places on our trip that Steven had not visited on his other journeys. He had met chef Duhul Safdi and heard that his whole roasted eggplant topped with hummus was legendary, and when we tasted it, we both heartily agreed. I had become obsessed with hummus. At the market stalls and at Abu Hasan in Jaffa, the hummus was unlike anything I had tasted—and enjoyed—in America. It was smooth and bursting with flavor and became a major part of my conversations on this trip. I think many people in Israel will remember me as "that lady who talked a lot about hummus." For my interpretation of Duhul's dish, I added zhug, za'atar, and torn fresh mint to take the eggplant even farther on up the flavor road. One of my top takeaways from the trip was the way fresh, torn herbs mixed with a sprinkling of zhug and za'atar bring brightness to a dish. To me, the brilliance of the new cuisine of Israel all comes together in this one simple dish. Everything other than the eggplant can be made in advance, and what is left over of the hummus, zhug, and za'atar can be used for other recipes in this book.

HUMMUS TAHINI

2 cups (400 g) dried chickpeas or garbanzo beans
¾ cup (180 ml) plus 1 tablespoon extra virgin olive oil, divided
¼ cup (75 g) kosher salt
1 large onion, peeled and quartered
1 large carrot, peeled and cut into thirds
1 large celery rib, cut into thirds
1 whole head garlic unpeeled, halved through the middle
5 fresh sage leaves
2 dried red arbol chilies
2 bay leaves
1 rosemary sprig
½ cup (120 g) tahini
1 tablespoon ice water
4 garlic cloves
Juice of 1 to 2 lemons, halved
Kosher salt
1 small bunch mint, leaves torn

FOR HUMMUS: Place chickpeas in a pot or bowl. Add enough water to cover, and let stand overnight.

Drain chickpeas and transfer to pot. Add enough water to cover chickpeas by 1½ inches (3.8 cm). Add ¼ cup (60 ml) olive oil and the next 9 ingredients and bring to a boil. Reduce heat and simmer until chickpeas are very tender and creamy, 1 to 2 hours (time will vary depending on freshness of chickpeas), adding more water as necessary.

Drain chickpeas, reserving 3¼ cups (760 ml) plus 1 tablespoon cooking liquid and cooked garlic. Discard remaining chickpea cooking liquid and ingredients. Set aside ¼ cup (50 g) cooked chickpeas. Squeeze cooked garlic from head halves into a blender. Add remaining chickpeas, reserved cooking liquid and remaining ½ cup (120 ml) olive oil to the blender; do not blend yet.

Place ½ cup (120 g) tahini in the bowl of a stand mixer fitted with a whisk attachment. Whisk tahini at high speed until slightly thickened, about 10 minutes. Add ice water and continue whisking until it is the consistency of peanut butter. Add whisked tahini to blender with chickpeas and purée until smooth. Transfer to a bowl. Grate garlic into the bowl. Add in the lemon juice to taste. Season with salt. Let stand until ready to use.

ZA'ATAR

1 cup (40 g) fresh thyme leaves, finely chopped, or ¾ cup (65 g) dried thyme, crumbled

1 cup (40 g) fresh oregano leaves, finely chopped, or ¾ cup (65 g) dried oregano, crumbled

¼ cup (36 g) natural sesame seeds

2 tablespoons plus 2 teaspoons ground sumac

2 tablespoons lemon peel grated on microplane

2½ teaspoons extra virgin olive oil

1½ teaspoons flaked sea salt (Maldon)

1 teaspoon kosher salt

½ teaspoon hot red chili flakes

ZHUG

15 cardamom pods

1½ tablespoons cumin seeds

1½ teaspoons whole black peppercorns

1½ teaspoons coriander seeds

5 fresh jalapeño chilies, seeded and finely chopped

5 fresh red Fresno chilies, seeded and finely chopped

2 to 4 garlic cloves grated

1½ cups (24 g) cilantro leaves, chopped

Pinch of kosher salt

½ cup (120 ml) extra virgin olive oil

½ cup (120 ml) fresh lemon juice

EGGPLANT

4 globe eggplants

Extra virgin olive oil

Kosher salt

FOR ZA'ATAR: Preheat the oven to 325°F (160°C).

If using fresh herbs, spread on a baking sheet and bake for 30 minutes. Cool completely, then transfer to an airtight container. If using dried herbs, place in an airtight container. Spread the sesame seeds on another baking sheet. Bake until fragrant and golden brown, 10 to 12 minutes. Cool completely, then transfer to the container with herbs. Add remaining 6 ingredients and stir well. Cover and store at room temperature until ready to use.

FOR ZHUG: Toast the cardamom, cumin, peppercorns, and coriander in a small heavy skillet over medium heat, stirring constantly until fragrant. Let cool. Transfer to a spice grinder and grind until powdery.

Place both chilies and garlic in a mortar. Add the ground toasted spices. Using a pestle, pound to a rough paste. Add cilantro and salt and mash together. Stir in the oil. Transfer to a bowl. Stir in the lemon juice and season with additional salt if desired. Let stand until ready to use.

FOR EGGPLANT: Preheat the oven to the highest setting, usually 450 or 500°F (230 or 260°C).

Slice a shallow slit in the eggplants from top to bottom to allow air to escape while roasting. Rub eggplants with the olive oil. Season with salt. Set on a baking sheet and bake until the flesh is soft and the skin is charred but not burned, 25 to 30 minutes; time will vary depending on the size of eggplants. Cover eggplants with plastic wrap and let stand until skin softens, 10 to 20 minutes.

Place eggplants on serving platters, opening each to expose the flesh. Top each eggplant with a spoonful of hummus, not covering the eggplant entirely. Drizzle with olive oil. Sprinkle generously with za'atar. Garnish with a spoonful of zhug. Season with salt. Sprinkle with reserved ¼ cup (50 g) cooked chickpeas and mint and serve.

Lebanese Fattoush Salad

Many guests arrive from Tel Aviv by helicopter to taste Joseph Hanna's refined Arab cuisine. The first time Dorit and I visited his restaurant, Magdalena, we arrived in my nondescript red rental car, but we probably enjoyed the same taste sensations as our more privileged dining companions when we ate this marvelous salad, seasoned with tangy sumac. I have since made this salad numerous times at home and it is always as pleasing as it was the first time I had it.

3 medium-size ripe tomatoes, cut into large chunks

3 medium cucumbers, cut into large chunks

4 large green onions, thinly sliced

3 medium radishes, thinly sliced

1/2 cup (20 g) flat-leaf parsley leaves

1/2 cup (20 g) mint leaves

1/4 cup (60 ml) fresh lemon juice

1/2 cup (120 ml) extra virgin olive oil

2 tablespoons ground sumac

Salt

2/3 cup (5.3 ounces; 150 g) whole milk ricotta cheese or buffalo mozzarella cheese, cut into chunks

2 pita breads, cut into pieces and toasted in oven

Place the tomatoes, cucumbers, green onions, and radishes in a large bowl. Sprinkle with the parsley and mint leaves. Pour the lemon juice over the salad. Drizzle with the olive oil. Sprinkle with the sumac. Toss, then season with salt to taste. Garnish with the cheese and toasted pita.

Nancy's Freekeh Tabouleh with Preserved Lemon Vinaigrette

One of the highlights of my trip with Steven was the opportunity to take a cooking class in the home of Nahida and Adnan Kavishi, a Druze couple who live in Julis in the Western Galilee. Nahida taught us how to stuff grape leaves and zucchini and to make F'tir and Baradeh. What stood out for me most was the flavor of the freekeh, a smoked green wheat. It looked like bulgur but had a much more pronounced and nutty flavor. When I ate it, my head started spinning. A spinning head is my single favorite response to a taste sensation, because it always signals inspiration. "This would be great in tabouleh," I mused. As my head spun at about 9,500 rpm, I recalled the combination of falafel with a slice of preserved lemon I had enjoyed just days before at the Akko market. I wanted to find a way to use preserved lemons in one of the recipes for this book and when I tasted the freekeh, I knew I had a lovely match. The lemons need to preserve for two to three days, so plan this recipe in advance.

1 scant cup (185 g) freekeh

1½ cups (350 ml) water

1 teaspoon kosher salt

2 tablespoons extra virgin olive oil

1 pound (450 g; about 5 bunches) flat-leaf parsley, stems removed, leaves chopped

Preserved Lemon Vinaigrette (see facing page)

1 pint (300 g) cherry tomatoes, halved through the stem

Salt and freshly ground pepper

Place the freekeh in a colander and rinse under cold water until water runs clear. Place 1½ cups (350 ml) water in a medium-size heavy saucepan and bring to a boil. Stir salt, then freekeh, into the boiling water and return water to boiling. Reduce heat to medium-low and simmer until freekeh is al dente and all water has been absorbed, 8 to 10 minutes depending on freshness of the freekeh.

Remove freekeh from heat and fluff with a fork. Transfer to a baking sheet and spread freekeh evenly. Refrigerate until room temperature to prevent stickiness. Remove from refrigerator. Drizzle with oil and toss with hands to thoroughly coat grains.

Transfer freekeh to a large bowl. Add the parsley and toss well. Toss with enough vinaigrette to ensure the grains are well moistened. Add the tomatoes and toss well. Season with salt and pepper. Add more vinaigrette if desired.

PRESERVED LEMON VINAIGRETTE

PRESERVED LEMONS

4 whole lemons, cut into ½-inch
 (13 mm) rounds
¼ cup (75 g) salt
1 teaspoon sugar
Olive oil

VINAIGRETTE

¼ cup (60 ml) fresh lemon juice
¼ cup (60 ml) Champagne vinegar
1 tablespoon minced shallot
1 tablespoon snipped chives
1½ teaspoons sugar
½ teaspoon hot red chili flakes
¼ cup finely chopped preserved
 lemon
1 cup extra virgin olive oil
Salt and freshly ground pepper

FOR LEMONS: Place lemons, salt, and sugar in a bowl. Toss until lemon slices are thoroughly covered with salt and sugar. Transfer lemons to a container. Pour in enough olive oil to cover lemons completely. Cover container and let stand at room temperature until lemons are soft but not mushy, and mellow in flavor, 2 to 3 days.

This makes more than you will need for the vinaigrette, but it keeps for a long time in the refrigerator and can be used on braised meat and grilled fish or chicken.

FOR VINAIGRETTE: Combine the lemon juice, vinegar, shallot, chives, sugar, and chili flakes in a bowl. Stir in the preserved lemon. Slowly whisk in the olive oil. Season with salt and pepper.

Sharabik

A few weeks after my first visit to Sharabik in Rameh, I returned there for lunch with Nancy. I had been talking about it nonstop for days, and when we arrived at the restaurant, I suddenly became afraid that I might have been too enthusiastic in my praise for the chef and his food and that Nancy would be disappointed. She wasn't. She sincerely appreciated the simple food and the humility of the owner, Yakub Hiat, who told her that he doesn't think of himself as a chef, "just a person who prepares food with simple techniques to preserve the true flavors of my ingredients."

While I photographed our two favorite dishes, Nancy, the scribe, with pen and paper in hand, sat down with him as he dictated his recipes. Nancy's suggestions are in brackets.

CAULIFLOWER WITH TART ORANGE SAUCE

Look for a cauliflower with lots of green leaves attached. Cut the cauliflower and its leaves into small chunks, but not too small. Season with [kosher] salt and, over a medium-high heat, fry the cauliflower chunks in olive oil until golden brown all over, stirring occasionally so they color evenly on all sides. Transfer them to a small dish, and spoon tahini that has been mixed with a few drops of lemon and ice water over the cauliflower. Using a not-too-sweet tangerine, orange, or mandarin—better if not even ripe—squeeze the juice over the top. If you buy the citrus at the farmers market, ask which variety is the sweetest and then buy the opposite.

EGGPLANT WITH POMEGRANATE REDUCTION

Choose a large round purple eggplant, preferably the huge baladi known as The Bags of Madame. Peel it and slice it in half lengthwise and then across in half-moons ¾ inch (2 cm) thick. Season the eggplant slices with [kosher] salt. Sauté them in olive oil on both sides until brown.

Transfer the eggplant to a platter. Squish them with a fork until smooth. [With a fine microplane, grate 2 garlic cloves directly into 2 tablespoons olive oil.] Drizzle the garlic oil onto the eggplant. Do not use too much garlic oil. Squeeze lemon on the eggplant. [With the back of a spoon,] paint the eggplant with tahini mixed with a few drops of lemon and ice water. Paint the top with pomegranate syrup* and garnish with torn mint leaves.

*Available at well-stocked Middle Eastern stores or online.

OVERLEAF: LANDSCAPE IN THE COUNTRYSIDE BETWEEN THE SEA OF GALILEE AND THE JORDANIAN BORDER.

Nancy's Cauliflower Focaccia

Steven was most excited for me to meet Erez Komarovsky. One of the reasons was because it had been the most difficult meeting for him to set up and it had become a challenge to even make it happen. The other was because Erez, like me, is a baker. He had once owned a few bakeries but had sold them and was now giving cooking classes in his home in the Western Galilee, a long drive from where we were staying in Zikhron Ya'akov. "This better be worth it," I told Steven about six or seven times. He insisted, with his unbridled enthusiasm, that it would be worth every kilometer. As soon as Erez opened the door to his home, I knew Steven had been right. The setting was majestic, the views were magnificent, and everything he served us, including the cauliflower focaccia that inspired this recipe, was beautiful and delicious. But most remarkable of all, for me, as a baker, was Erez's focaccia, which show-cased so sublimely the wonder of transformation that an oven can bring about. Here was a clump, an ungraceful, oddball looking vegetable, that went into the oven and came out transformed into something beautiful. The oven is the world's greatest makeup artist.

FOCACCIA SPONGE

1/2 scant cup (120 ml) water

1/8 scant packed teaspoon cake yeast
   or 1/16 teaspoon active dry yeast

1/2 cup (70 g) plus 3 tablespoons
   bread flour

FOCACCIA DOUGH

Olive oil (for greasing bowl)

1 1/4 cups (300 ml) plus
   2 tablespoons water

1 scant tablespoon olive oil

3 1/3 (450 g) cups bread flour

2 tablespoons plus 3/4 teaspoon
   rye flour

2 packed tablespoons plus 1/4 packed
   teaspoon fresh cake yeast or
   1 3/4 teaspoons active dry yeast

1 tablespoon kosher salt

Additional bread flour

1/2 cup (120 ml) olive oil (for
   greasing pans)

(continued)

FOR SPONGE: Pour the water into a small plastic or ceramic bowl. Sprinkle the yeast over the water. Let stand until water has absorbed the yeast, a few minutes. Using a wooden spoon, stir in the bread flour and continue stirring until well combined. Cover the top of the bowl with plastic wrap, then wrap sides of the bowl with plastic wrap. Let stand at room temperature (preferably 68 to 70°F; 20 to 21°C) until bubbly, thick, and the texture of wallpaper paste (thicker than pancake batter but thinner than dough), 12 to 24 hours.

FOR DOUGH: Using olive oil, lightly grease a bowl large enough to hold the dough when it has doubled in size. Transfer the sponge to the bowl of a stand mixer fitted with a dough hook. Add the water and olive oil. Add the bread flour, rye flour, and yeast and mix on low speed until ingredients are thoroughly combined and the dough comes together, about 2 minutes. With the mixer running, slowly beat in the salt. Increase speed to medium and continue mixing until the dough is smooth, well formed, and starts to pull away from the sides of the bowl, 6 to 8 minutes. (Please note that the dough will not "clean" the bowl, but if dough is too sticky and not pulling away from

(continued)

Cauliflower Focaccia (continuation)

the sides, add some additional bread flour, 1 tablespoon at a time, to achieve desired consistency.) Transfer dough to the prepared bowl. Cover top of the bowl with plastic wrap, then wrap sides of bowl with plastic wrap. Let stand at room temperature until doubled in volume, about $1\frac{1}{2}$ hours.

Turn dough out onto a lightly floured work surface. Proceeding as if dough round has four sides, fold the edges toward the center. Turn dough over and return it to the bowl, folded sides down. Cover top of the bowl with plastic wrap; wrap the sides with plastic wrap. Let stand at room temperature for 50 to 60 minutes. The dough should feel alive, springy, and resistant and should not collapse when touched.

Position the rack in the center of the oven and preheat oven to 450°F (230°C).

Pour $\frac{1}{4}$ cup (60 ml) olive oil into each of two 10 x 2-inch (25 x 5 cm) round cake pans. Tilt pans to coat the bottoms evenly with oil. Gently turn dough out onto a lightly floured work surface; do not deflate the dough. Divide dough into two even pieces. Place into prepared pans. Gently pull edges of the dough to obtain a roughly round shape. Cover pans with clean dishcloths and let stand at room temperature until dough is relaxed and covers half the surface of the pans, about 30 minutes.

GARNISH

¼ cup (60 ml) olive oil

2 medium heads cauliflower, trimmed and cut into 4 wedges each

Kosher salt

2 ounces (60 g) low-moisture mozzarella, cut into generous ½-inch (1 cm) cubes

Olive oil (for brushing focaccias)

FOR GARNISH: Meanwhile, heat the olive oil in a large heavy skillet over medium-high heat. Sprinkle the cauliflower wedges with salt. Add them to the skillet and sear 3 minutes on each side. Transfer to a baking sheet and let cool.

Divide the mozzarella cubes between focaccias and arrange evenly over the dough. Push the cubes deeply into the dough so they are almost flush with the surface. Simultaneously push the dough outward to encourage it toward the edges of the pans. Arrange 4 cauliflower wedges atop each focaccia and push them gently into the dough. Let stand at room temperature for 15 to 20 minutes.

TO BAKE AND SERVE: Bake the focaccias until they are crisp, golden brown, and have almost risen to the tops of the pans, 30 to 40 minutes. Set pans on the bottom of the oven and bake until bottoms of the focaccias are crisp and golden brown, about 5 minutes.

Using a fork as an aide, immediately transfer focaccias from pans to wire racks to cool; be careful of any hot oil still at the bottoms of pans. Brush surfaces of focaccias with olive oil and set aside to cool.

Transfer focaccias to a cutting board. Cut each into quarters and serve immediately. (If not eating immediately, wait to cut.)

Challah with Olives, Anchovies, and Oregano

This challah, the cover image of *Israel Eats*, was sitting on a low wood table when Nancy and I arrived at Erez Komarovsky's home in Mattat. He refers to it as a "salty yeast cake," and it truly melts in your mouth. The dough needs to rise overnight in the refrigerator, so please plan ahead for this tour de force.

6 cups (750 g) all-purpose flour

3 tablespoons sugar

2½ teaspoons Red Star Platinum Yeast or other active dry yeast

½ teaspoon salt

1 egg, beaten

1 to 1½ (240 to 350 ml) cups water

1 cup (2 sticks; 240 g) butter, chilled, cut into squares

1 to 2 (2-ounce; 60 g) cans anchovies (preferably Spanish or Portuguese), drained but not rinsed, chopped

½ cup (90 g) coarsely chopped pitted kalamata olives

1½ tablespoons fresh oregano leaves

GUY SHAMIR AND HIS DAUGHTER, MEYO, TAKING A BREAK FROM THE OLIVE HARVEST IN CLIL.

Combine the flour, sugar, yeast, and salt in the large bowl of a stand mixer fitted with a bread hook. Make a well in the center. Add the egg and 1 cup (240 ml) of the water to the well; mix on low speed until the dough starts to hold together but is not too wet or too dry; add up to ½ cup (120 ml) water if necessary. Gradually mix in the butter and continue mixing until the dough becomes smooth and elastic. Oil a large bowl. Transfer dough to the oiled bowl. Cover and refrigerate to rise overnight.

Transfer dough to a floured work surface and punch down, then roll out into a rectangle approximately 15 to 18 inches (40 to 45 cm) long and 8 to 10 inches (20 to 25 cm) wide. Press the anchovies, olives, and oregano into the dough. Cut the rectangle into 3 even strips. Set strips on a pastry board or a long sheet of parchment paper. Take 1 strip of the dough and gently flip it over so the anchovy- and olive-studded surface is face down. Using clean hands and starting from the middle and working outward, roll dough away from you into a strand that is approximately 18 to 20 inches (45 to 50 cm) long with a 1-inch (2.5 cm) diameter. Keep the strand as even as possible. Set first strand aside and repeat to make 2 more strands of equal length. To braid, lay the strands side by side and start from the center: grab the bottom edge of the right strand and bring over the center strand so it crosses at the middle, making that strand the center strand. Bring the left strand over that strand. Repeat until the end is reached. Pinch ends together and tuck them under the braid. Turn the pastry board or parchment paper around and repeat the process with the other half of the braid. Cover the challah and let it stand at room temperature until doubled in volume, 1½ to 2 hours.

Preheat oven to 350°F (175°C). Set challah on a baking sheet and bake until golden brown, about 40 minutes. (As ovens vary, start checking the bread at 25 minutes and then every 5 minutes until the bread is golden brown.) Let cool completely before slicing.

F'tir

Nancy and I spent an interesting morning cooking with Nahida and Adnan Kavishi, our Druze hosts in the town of Julis. Nahida was happily stuffing these marvelous savory pastries and chatting about having lost three of her seven sons, and then her husband, which confused me because he was standing next to me. After a few minutes of listening to her conversation, I realized that she was referring to a past life. The Druze believe in reincarnation and feel very comfortable reminiscing about any one of their lives. Nahida zeroed in on our former lives and began to tell us about them. I mentioned that I was having enough of a challenge making sense of this one and did not wish to add to my confusion. These pastries are traditionally cooked on a saj, like the one in the photograph of the Majdal Shams bakery on page 4.

DOUGH

2 cups (250 g) whole-wheat flour

2 cups (250 g) all-purpose flour

1 teaspoon instant dry yeast

1 teaspoon salt

1 cup (240 ml) olive oil

1 cup (240 ml) (about) water

FILLING

1 large bunch Swiss chard or large-
    leaf spinach, stems removed,
    leaves thinly sliced

1 large onion, diced

3 tablespoons olive oil

Salt and freshly ground pepper

FOR DOUGH: Place both flours in a large bowl. Add the yeast and mix well to combine. Add the salt and mix well to combine. Make a well in the center of the flour. Add the oil to the well and stir, using a wooden spoon to incorporate the flour into the oil. Stir in enough water to make a smooth dough. Turn dough out onto a floured work surface and knead for 15 minutes; it should be soft and even smoother. Cover and let stand in a warm, draft-free area for 15 minutes.

FOR FILLING: Combine all ingredients in a large bowl.

TO ASSEMBLE: Divide dough into 10 equal-size portions. Roll out each portion into an 8-inch (20 cm) round that is ¼ inch (6 mm) thick. Spoon 2 generous tablespoons of the filling onto half of each round, leaving a border. Fold dough over to enclose the filling. Crimp the edges with a fork. Set dough on parchment or waxed paper. Repeat with the remaining rounds and filling. (Do not let the pastries touch each other while waiting to be cooked or the dough will rip.)

TO COOK: Lightly oil a large heavy skillet and heat over medium heat until hot. Add the pastries to the pan—do not crowd—and cook the first sides until it is slightly crispy, about 5 minutes. Turn the pastries over and cook for 3 minutes on the second sides. Serve immediately.

Galilean Kugel

Erez Komarovsky loves kugel. His Polish grandmother used to make it for him and he decided to play with her old recipe, give it a renaissance, and create a new, sacrilegious tension between tradition and bacon. He told me that kugel is only alive in the orthodox societies where they put it in the oven on Friday night, cook it for ten hours, and eat it on Saturday morning, so please plan in advance, dust off your *kugelhopf* or fluted tube pan, and get to work.

$\frac{1}{2}$ cup (70 g) golden raisins

$\frac{1}{4}$ cup (60 ml) Arak or other anise-flavored spirit, such as Sambuca

1 pound (450 g) spaghetti noodles

1 pound (450 g) bacon, cut into small pieces

1 cup (240 ml) sunflower or peanut oil

1 cup (200 g) sugar

1 teaspoon coarsely ground black pepper

1 teaspoon coarsely ground white pepper

Sea salt

OVERLEAF, LEFT: MUNTAHA NAAM, FORAGER IN AKKO. **OVERLEAF, RIGHT:** CHEF MICHAEL GROTOFSKY, OWNER OF BISTRO MICHAEL IN LIMAN, WHO TOLD ME HIS CAREER IS NOT HIS LIFE, HIS LIFE IS HIS CAREER.

Preheat oven to 200°F (90°C). Lightly grease a standard kugelhopf pan or fluted tube pan (about $9\frac{1}{2}$ inches; 24 cm).

Place the raisins in a small bowl. Pour the Arak over raisins and let stand until ready to use.

Bring a large pot of salted water to a boil. Add the noodles and cook until tender but still firm to bite; do not overcook. Drain the noodles.

Meanwhile, place the bacon in a large heavy skillet and cook until crispy. Pour off the bacon fat. Stir noodles into the bacon. Drain the raisins; stir raisins into the bacon.

Combine the oil and sugar in a small heavy saucepan over medium heat and cook, swirling the pan and washing down the sides of the pan with a pastry brush dipped in water so crystals do not form. Do not overcook the caramel or it will burn. Stir caramel into the noodle mixture. Stir in both peppers and season to taste with salt. Transfer to the prepared pan. Cover with aluminum foil. Bake for 10 hours. Unmold onto a platter and serve.

Kohlrabi and Carrot Salad

8 SERVINGS

This salad is served as part of the sumptuous breakfast spread at Mitzpe Hayamim in Rosh Pina. When the restaurant's doors open at 7:30 a.m. and the guests are allowed in, the experience is similar to being on the red carpet with the incessant camera flashes of the paparazzi. Everyone wants to remember this breakfast. One morning, standing in front of tables laden with everything a person could wish for, I overheard a guest ask for corn flakes.

2 medium kohlrabi, peeled and grated
4 medium carrots, peeled and grated
1/2 cup (20 g) chopped fresh cilantro
1/2 cup (20 g) chopped flat-leaf parsley
1/4 cup (60 ml) freshly squeezed lemon juice
Salt and freshly ground pepper
Pinch of sugar (optional)

Mix the kohlrabi, carrots, cilantro, parsley, and lemon juice in a large serving bowl. Season with salt and pepper. Add a pinch of sugar if desired. Serve immediately.

Sweet Pumpkin, Pecan, and Raisin Salad

4 TO 6 SERVINGS

The pumpkin is raw in Mitzpe Hayamim's breakfast salad. There is an interesting interplay between the spicy sauce, the sweet ingredients, and the squash's texture. I imagined it at Thanksgiving next to thick slices of turkey.

1 pound (450 g) pumpkin or butternut squash, peeled and grated
2/3 cup (80 g) pecan pieces
1/2 cup (120 ml) fresh orange juice
1/4 cup (40 g) dark raisins or currants
2 tablespoons honey
1 tablespoon firmly packed dark brown sugar
1 teaspoon (or more) green hot pepper sauce, such as green Tabasco
Salt and freshly ground pepper

Mix the first 6 ingredients in a large serving bowl. Add 1 teaspoon of hot pepper sauce. Adjust the seasoning with additional hot pepper sauce if desired and salt and pepper. Serve immediately or let stand and serve later.

THE BREAKFAST SALADS AT MITZPE HAYAMIM. KOHLRABI AND CARROT SALAD IS FOURTH FROM THE TOP. SWEET PUMPKIN, PECAN, AND RAISIN SALAD IS FIFTH FROM TOP.

Kubbeh with Chickpeas, Pine Nuts, and Halloumi Cheese

MAKES APPROXIMATELY 4 DOZEN

This vegetarian version of kubbeh, normally a meat-filled dumpling, but here stuffed with chickpeas and cheese, is my idea of heaven. True to his word, Joseph Hanna, chef/owner of Magdalena restaurant, has elevated a classic Levantine recipe into something delicate and refined. Serve them drizzled with tahini or with Yogurt, Walnut, and Horseradish Dip (page 88).

DOUGH

1 pound (450 g) fine bulgur cracked wheat

3 cups (700 ml) water

1 teaspoon salt

1 teaspoon smoked paprika

1/2 teaspoon ground cinnamon

1/2 teaspoon ground allspice

1/4 teaspoon ground nutmeg

Water

Unseasoned dry breadcrumbs

FILLING

1 cup (200 g) dried chickpeas (also called garbanzo beans), picked through

2 quarts (2 l) water

1/2 cup (120 ml) olive oil

1 large onion, chopped

4 large garlic cloves, chopped

1/2 cup (70 g) small pine nuts, toasted

1 tablespoon fresh lemon juice

2 teaspoons ground cumin

1 teaspoon salt

1/4 teaspoon ground allspice

1/8 teaspoon ground nutmeg

(continued)

FOR DOUGH: Place bulgur in a bowl. Cover with hot water. Let stand for 30 minutes.

Remove any excess water from the bulgur by squeezing it with your hands, then transfer it to a food processor. Add the salt and spices. Pulse until ingredients come together and the dough is easy to work with. If the mixture is too dry to hold together, add water, 2 tablespoons at a time, until it becomes a workable dough. If mixture is too wet, add enough breadcrumbs to achieve a workable dough. Do not overmix; you want a somewhat grainy texture. Transfer dough to a bowl. Cover and refrigerate for 1 hour.

FOR FILLING: Place the chickpeas in a large pot. Add water. Bring to a boil over high heat and cook for 2 to 3 minutes. Remove from heat. Let stand for 1 hour.

Drain chickpeas and rinse thoroughly with cold water. Transfer them to a food processor. Pulse until coarsely chopped, about 8 to 10 times.

Heat the olive oil in a large heavy skillet over medium heat. Add the onion and sauté until translucent, about 5 minutes. Add the coarsely chopped chickpeas and the garlic and cook, stirring occasionally, until chickpeas are halfway cooked, about 20 minutes. (Add a bit of water if mixture is too dry.) Stir in the pine nuts, lemon juice, cumin, salt, allspice, and nutmeg. Stir in the cheese and coriander.

½ cup (70 g) finely diced halloumi
   cheese
¼ cup (10 g) chopped coriander or
   parsley leaves
Vegetable oil (for deep-frying)

TO ASSEMBLE: Form the dough into ping pong ball–size rounds, squeezing the mixture first to compact the dough so it is not too loose. Keep a small bowl of cold water at the ready to dip your fingers in between forming croquettes to prevent dough from becoming too sticky. Holding the first dough ball in one hand, use the index finger of your other hand to form a well in the center of the round. Press one finger toward the bottom of the ball but do not poke through. Press your finger against the sides of the well to form thin walls. Spoon 1½ teaspoons of the filling into the round. Seal the end by tapering the dough closed and form another taper at the opposite end to create the croquette shape. Repeat instructions above for each remaining dough round. Place the filled kubbeh on a tray or platter in a single layer.

TO FRY: Heat the oil to 350°F (175°C) in a large heavy pot or deep fryer. Cook the kubbeh in batches (do not crowd) until golden brown, about 3 minutes. Using a slotted utensil, remove kubbeh from the oil and transfer to paper towels to drain. Serve hot or at room temperature.

Knafeh Akko Style

Knafeh might be the Arab world's most prominent comfort food dessert. Throughout Israel, there are bakeries and stands selling slices cut from two-foot-wide pans that women in chadors, businessmen in suits, and children with fists full of shekels line up to buy and devour right on the spot. I arrived very late to my appointment with Alaa Muse, chef and owner of El Marsa restaurant in Akko, and he was visibly unhappy about it, even though I had warned him in advance that I might not reach him by our appointed time. I asked him if he would like to swear at me in Hebrew or Arabic and a smile replaced his frown as he replied, "Arabic, because there are more dirty words." He invited me to sit down and we shared one of his perfect knafeh, becoming fast friends as the forkfuls of the sweet cheese dessert worked their magic.

SUGAR SYRUP

2 cups (400 g) sugar

1½ cups (13 ounces; 375 ml) water

½ small lemon, sliced

1 small cinnamon stick

3 cardamom pods

3 cloves

1 star anise pod

PASTRY

8 ounces (200 g) kadaif pastry
  (shredded phyllo pastry)

4 tablespoons (2 ounces; 50 g)
  clarified butter

1¼ cups (10½ ounces; 300 g)
  whole milk ricotta cheese

¼ cup (30 g) chopped toasted
  peeled pistachios

FOR SUGAR SYRUP: Place the sugar in a medium-size heavy saucepan over medium-low heat and cook, stirring occasionally, until sugar becomes a dark amber color, 8 to 12 minutes. Add the water, lemon, and spices and bring to a boil. (Please note that the sugar will seize and harden as soon as the water is added. It will begin to melt as the mixture comes to a boil.) Reduce heat and simmer for 10 minutes. Remove from heat and let the syrup stand for 5 minutes, then strain. Measure out 1 cup (240 ml) of syrup for this dish (reserve remainder for another use). Keep the 1 cup (240 ml) syrup hot.

FOR PASTRY: Place the kadaif pastry in a bowl. Using clean hands, separate the large clumps and break the shreds into smaller pieces. Melt 2 tablespoons clarified butter and drizzle it over the pastry. Using your hands, mix the butter into the pastry. Rub the remaining 2 tablespoons clarified butter over the bottom and sides of an 8-inch (20 cm) nonstick skillet. Place the kadaif in the skillet, pressing down to form an even ½-inch (13 mm) thick layer. Using a silicone or rubber spatula, spread the cheese over the kadaif. Set the skillet on medium-low heat and cook until kadaif is browned, rotating skillet constantly for even browning. Invert contents of skillet onto a platter. Immediately ladle the hot spiced sugar syrup evenly over the pastry. Sprinkle with the chopped pistachios. Cut into 4 wedges and serve.

Magic Kesem Crackers

MAKES ABOUT 56 (2 X 2-INCH; 5 X 5 CM) CRACKERS

When friends on the Ashram in southern Israel, where Hagit Lidror first began cooking, tasted these crackers, they would say, "Wow they're magical!" Hagit now lives in Clil, where she operates culinary workshops she calls "Cooking as a Way of Living." By trial and error, Hagit learned how to cook vegetarian food and, as she describes it, "like a river that suddenly flows, cooking flew out of me." Try these crackers with her Fresh Za'atar Spread (page 91).

3 cups (270 g) spelt, rye, or whole-wheat flour, plus more for kneading

1 cup (140 g) raw unsalted sunflower seeds

1 cup (160 g) sesame seeds

1 cup (170 g) flax seeds

1 cup (80 g) rolled oats

1 teaspoon kosher salt

1 cup (240 ml) extra virgin olive oil

2 to 3 cups (475 to 700 ml) water

Combine the 3 cups flour, all the seeds, oats, and salt in a large bowl. Make a well in the center. Add the oil to the well and stir with a wooden spoon to blend together. Gradually stir in enough water to make a sticky dough (start with 2 cups; 475 ml); the amount of water needed will vary depending on the flour used and the weather. Turn the dough out onto a floured work surface and knead briefly until it is elastic, adding a bit more flour if necessary.

Preheat the oven to 350°F (175°C).

Place a large sheet of parchment paper on your work surface. Using wet, clean hands, transfer dough from the bowl to parchment paper. Grease another sheet of parchment paper and place it greased-side down atop the dough. Using a rolling pin, roll dough out until it is $1/16$ inch (1.5 mm) thick. Remove top piece of parchment. Using a pizza cutter or a wet, sharp knife, cut dough into 2 x 2-inch (5 x 5 cm) pieces. Place the pieces of dough on a baking sheet. Bake until crisp and brown, 30 to 40 minutes. Cool the crackers completely. Store in an airtight container.

Kumquat Marmalade

On a gray, wet morning at the Pausa Inn in the Golan Heights, Einat Rothem served me this sublime marmalade. I was dazzled by its jewel-like appearance, and when I took my first taste, Gentile da Fabriano's masterpiece *Adoration of the Magi* immediately flashed in my mind. Was I eating the raiment of the Magi for breakfast?

2 pounds (1 kg) kumquats

4¼ cups (2 pounds; 1 kg) sugar

½ cup (120 ml) water

3 tablespoons lemon juice

Using a sharp knife, make a slot along each kumquat and remove the seeds. Place kumquats in a large heavy pot. Cover with water, bring to a boil, and let boil for 3 minutes. Drain kumquats and rinse them thoroughly with cold water.

Return kumquats to the pot. Add the sugar and water and cook over low heat until sugar is completely dissolved.

When the sugar has dissolved, increase heat and bring the sugar water to a boil. Boil for 1 minute, then reduce heat to the lowest setting and cook for 45 minutes, stirring frequently. Add the lemon juice and continue cooking over very low heat, stirring frequently, until the kumquats just turn amber in color, about 30 minutes.

If storing, transfer the hot marmalade to sterilized jars, then cover and boil the jars according to standard canning directions. If using immediately, transfer marmalade to a glass bowl, let cool, then cover and refrigerate.

Date Honey and Tahini Semifreddi with Cashew Brittle

The inventive use of tahini in Israeli cuisine fascinates me. I stayed a few nights at Smadar and Yossi Yardeni's B+B in Clil, where Smadar finished off the meal with this pleasing balance of sweet, nutty, and frozen sensations. Silan is often called date honey and is a brown syrup extracted from dates. It can be found in Middle Eastern markets, or you can make it yourself following the step-by-step pictures and detailed instructions on blogger Tori Avey's website, www.ToriAvey.com.

SEMIFREDDI

2 (14-ounce; 400 ml) cans coconut cream

1 cup (240 g) raw tahini

1/2 cup (120 ml) (or more) silan (date honey)

CASHEW BRITTLE

2 heaping tablespoons muscovado sugar

4 tablespoons water

12 raw cashew nuts, roughly chopped

FOR SEMIFREDDI: Refrigerate the cans of coconut cream for at least 3 hours or overnight to separate the fat from the liquid.

Open cans and scoop out the fat that has risen to the top and place it in a bowl. (Reserve remaining liquid for another use, such as cooking rice or making curries.) Using a hand-held electric mixer or a balloon whisk, beat the coconut cream solids until the mixture reaches the texture of whipped cream. Fold in the tahini and silan. (Taste and add more silan if desired.) Transfer the mixture to silicone molds that have a 3-inch (7.6 cm) radius or a 6-inch (15 cm) diameter. Freeze until set or overnight. (You can also use similar-size custard cups or a 9 x 5-inch [23 x 13 cm] loaf pan, but make sure to line them with plastic wrap for easy unmolding.)

FOR BRITTLE: Combine the sugar and water in a small heavy saucepan over medium-high heat and bring to a boil. Continue cooking until sugar dissolves, stirring and brushing down the sides of the pan with a wet pastry brush to prevent sugar crystals from forming. Reduce heat and simmer without stirring, swirling pan occasionally, until the caramel is golden around the edges, about 8 minutes. Remove from heat and stir in the nuts. Spread thinly and evenly on a silicone mat or a greased baking sheet and cool completely. Snap the brittle into pieces or crumble into small bits.

Unmold the semifreddi onto plates. Garnish with the brittle pieces or bits.

Vegan Chocolate Mint Cake

By the age of twelve, Hagit Lidror was baking all her family's birthday cakes. When I visited her at her home in Clil, she told me I had to taste this cake before she would tell me what was in it because, she said, "you should never tell anyone that they are about to eat an avocado cake." Make sure to start preparing this cake at least one day before you plan to serve it. If you freeze it, it will taste like ice cream. "Unusual and adventurous," said her son's guitar teacher, who tasted it with me. I have never been a connoisseur of cakes, but, being a lover of anything with fresh almonds or avocados, I was completely won over by this one.

CAKE BASE

1½ (180 g) cups mixed raw nuts (walnuts, pecans, almonds, and hazelnuts)

1 cup (150 g) pitted soft dates

¼ cup (28 g) unsweetened cocoa powder

2 tablespoons melted coconut oil

½ teaspoon vanilla extract

Pinch of salt

FILLING

2 large ripe avocados

½ cup (120 ml) melted coconut oil

¼ cup (60 ml) agave syrup

1 tablespoon mint leaves

2 teaspoons mint extract

1 teaspoon fresh lemon juice

Pinch of salt

CHOCOLATE CREAM

½ (55 g) cup unsweetened cocoa powder

¼ cup (60 ml) agave syrup

2 tablespoons almond milk or water

2 tablespoons melted coconut oil

1 tablespoon vanilla extract

Pinch of salt

FOR CAKE BASE: Place the nuts in a bowl. Cover with water and let stand 1 hour or up to overnight. Drain.

Place the soaked and drained nuts in a food processor. Add the remaining ingredients and pulse to create a thick paste. Spread paste on the bottom of an 8-inch (20 cm) springform pan. Refrigerate.

FOR FILLING: Peel and seed the avocados and place them in a food processor. Add the remaining ingredients and pulse until blended and creamy. Pour the mixture over the cake base and spread evenly. Refrigerate for at least 4 hours.

FOR CREAM: Combine all ingredients in the top of a double boiler or in a metal bowl. Set the top of the double boiler or bowl over a pan of simmering water; do not let bottom of pan touch the water. Stir until the mixture is creamy, about 1 minute. Pour mixture over the filling. Refrigerate for another 4 hours.

GARNISH

½ cup (60 g) raw pistachios, finely
    chopped or ground
Chopped fresh mint leaves

FOR GARNISH: Set the cake on a platter. Gently remove springform sides. Scatter the pistachios and chopped mint leaves over the cake. Slice to serve.

SPRING ALMONDS.

THE CENTER

ON MY FIRST NIGHT IN ISRAEL, Dorit took me to Crusaders restaurant at the ancient port of Caesarea. We sat at a table under the stars looking out at the dark, swirling sea and watching the fishermen at work. This was my First Supper, and at that meal, I learned one of the most salient facts about Israeli cuisine: it is nirvana for salad lovers. I ate ten of them, possibly more, and didn't stop until the grilled, freshly caught fish arrived. We feasted for hours.

Moshe Ben Naim, the owner of Crusaders, reminds me of the Hollywood stereotype of a Mafia Don. Friends walk into the restaurant, head straight to his corner table to kiss him and exchange a few words, and then they leave. He learned to cook from the original owner of the restaurant, and after fifteen years of working there, he bought it. During our meeting, Moshe told me with pride that Crusaders was not a chef restaurant, but "a simple, fresh taste by the sea." His seafood comes primarily from his own fishing boat, and people tell him they love what's he's doing and to never change. Eighty percent of Moshe's business is made up of return customers from all over Israel—understandable, given his prime location on a historic port at the edge of the sea. "If I don't see Caesarea I become crazy," he confides. "When I travel, I tell my wife I want to press a button and be home now."

Caesarea is a wealthy, gated enclave with a village atmosphere that shares the coast with King Herod's ancient city Caesarea Maritima. A 2,000-year-old aqueduct running along the sea passes in the distance by Dorit's windows and is an impressive monument to look at first thing in the morning. And so is the inside of Dorit's refrigerator: the diversity of products and their freshness rivals any of the *shuks*, or markets, throughout the country. Every morning, Dorit leaves the house early to swim in the ocean and reappears a few hours later with more food: containers of marinated salmon, hummus mesabacha (called killer hummus by the Israelis because some of the chickpeas are left whole and it's served with a spicy sauce), and tahini; bricks of creamy feta; avocados; and heads of garlic that she conserves herself to slather on everything she eats.

When her children are home or friends are visiting, she miraculously has eggplants stuffed, chickens and cauliflower roasting in the oven, and salads in ornate bowls on the big round table in the center of her kitchen, with its turquoise walls and old Iranian ceramic tiles. I begged her to share some of her recipes with me but she repeatedly refused and told me that her friend Smadar was a better cook.

No one taught Smadar Vardi how to cook. "I read, I travel, I ask, I want to learn." She agreed to prepare charaima for me, a fish dish that is in the DNA of all Moroccan Jews living in Israel. The flavors are marvelously complex, with the smoky taste of the paprika, the spiciness of the chilies, and the freshness of the cilantro all in well-balanced harmony. Every family has a different version, depending on what village they're from, and every family recipe differs from grandmother to daughter to granddaughter. "Every Friday we eat this dish. If I don't make it one week, there is no Friday. Something is missing," Smadar told me. When she and her family lived in Prague for five years, it was difficult to find fresh fish there, so she drove six hours to Hamburg to get it.

After months of trying to pin her down (one of her three sons was always home on leave from the army), she finally agreed to make it for me on the Shabbat following Passover. The caveat was that I needed to buy the fish because it was Saturday and all her Jewish suppliers were closed. Dorit and I went to Faredis, Paradise in Arabic, an Arab town northeast of Caesarea to buy the fish. I never realized that a culinary symbiosis existed between the Arabs and Jews until we needed an ingredient on the Sabbath when all the Jewish businesses were closed.

Faredis was swarming with Jews shopping for their Sabbath meal. After we found the fish, we went into a market with a dirt floor and a rustic kitchen in the back, where women were stuffing grape leaves, frying falafel balls, and rolling out fresh pita stuffed with spinach. We greeted the cooks, and I looked around to see where they were baking the pitas. Out the kitchen door and to the left was a magnificent wood-burning oven with vertical slots on either side to contain the flaming embers. It was a hot morning, but the bakers in their head scarves and black robes seemed unfazed by the heat. We ate the hot, stuffed pita while we shopped, and Dorit bought some falafel and a few extra pitas in case we became famished on the ride home. I bought her a gigantic braid of fresh garlic for two dollars that would have cost at least thirty euros in France. Even after we took it into the house, the garlic's lingering perfume permeated the car interior for days. I loved driving around Israel smelling it. It reminded me of my father and his custom of having a small plate of chopped garlic with every meal.

The day before I photographed Smadar's charaima, Dorit suggested we go to Borkin's Breads in Binyamina to buy a few challahs to dip into the rich, spicy sauce. We entered the bakery and were overwhelmed by the fragrance of freshly baked bread. As I scanned the shelves overflowing with the meticulously displayed loaves, I had an inexplicable sense of déja vu.

Dorit is proud and supportive of my book project and promotes me whenever she can. She often uses the Hebrew word *slicha*, which means "excuse me," and it is one of the handiest things I learned in Israel. Whenever I hear it come out of her mouth, I am curious to know what she will be asking for. "What did you *slicha* about?" I asked. "I told them you are a world-famous photographer from the United States doing a book about the food of Israel and that you wanted to meet the owner."

Dorit's *slicha* resulted in Eran Borkin bursting out of the kitchen and vigorously shaking my hand. He is a solid, slightly scruffy man with a doughy heart and a huge amount of passion. We talked about his bakery and about my book, and then I asked him if he had ever heard of Nancy Silverton, a bread baker from Los Angeles. "Of course I have!" he exclaimed. "She is the reason I changed my life to become a baker!" I suddenly realized why the place felt familiar to me. The breads resembled Nancy's. I asked him if he had her books and when he said yes, I told him that I had photographed them. He fell silent and, like a man possessed, began filling my arms with bread.

A few months later, Eran and I worked together in his bakery. He told me that before he became a baker, he had started working as a photographer but felt restless until he discovered cooking. As a young chef, he had believed the more ingredients he put on the plate, the better any dish would taste. When he started reading haiku poetry, he changed his approach and became a minimalist. He took flour and the few additional ingredients needed to create something living, and made a new product— bread. He has been baking since 1995 and said he is still practicing, learning, and improving.

I took Nancy to meet Eran a few weeks after our shoot and the three of us sat and talked like old friends. He was proud to show her his bakery and Nancy was sincerely touched by his adulation. A few times he turned to me, startled, and murmured, "I can't believe this." When we left, he gave us a box of breads, containers of his salads, and some pastries and cakes. I was concerned that it wouldn't

all fit in the car. He took pictures of Nancy and me, I took pictures of him with Nancy, and when we finished, he walked away with his hands covering his face, still in disbelief.

One late afternoon, Dorit and I were driving around the wine region of Zichron Ya'acov photographing landscapes. We passed a dramatic-looking building with views of the ocean and learned it was a hotel with a newly opened restaurant. We decided to return to Zichron Ya'acov on our next free night and try it. We continued our drive down a narrow lane next to an open field. I looked out the window and noticed a couple walking their dog. I was drawn to their kind, open faces. The man had a perceptible sweetness and warmth, and the woman had a friendly, round, olive-skinned face and a curly gray bob. Dorit slowed down, I said shalom, and we pulled over and parked. The four of us started talking and the man remarked that it was one of the most beautiful skies in days. He told us he watches the sky because he is a paraglider and retired air force F-14 pilot. I told them about my book and asked if I could photograph them in the golden light and they agreed. When we finished their portrait, the couple, Benny and Ruthie Ben Israel, invited us to their home for a glass of wine. The wine couldn't possibly be served by itself, so out came four different varieties of cheese, two more local wines, warm bread, cucumbers, cherry tomatoes, fresh butter, and Benny's homemade pesto.

Both Benny and Ruthie are immersed in Israel's food and wine culture. Benny believes that there are no culinary traditions in Israel and that this is an advantage. "It gives us the opportunity to create something new," he told me. He also said that with this awareness Israel is on the threshold of a deeper appreciation and organization of its local products and cuisine, and is moving toward creating a system of controlled appellations similar to what France and Italy have done.

Ruthie is a sommelier and the founder of Wine and Plenty, a festival that showcases local artisanal producers of wine, olive oil, cheese, and breads. It is held in the early spring at the Memorial Gardens of Ramat Hanadiv, where Baron Edmond de Rothschild and his wife, Adelaide, were buried after they were moved from the Pere Lachaise Cemetery in Paris. I organized one of my trips to coincide with the festival and enjoyed milling around with the Israeli foodies and tasting the local wines.

The crowd at Wine and Plenty was a chic group of locals who had no inhibitions about pushing their way through the throng of people to sample the delicious products. Masik Kibbutz Magal presented an extensive display of their olive oils at the festival, and I tasted all twelve outstanding varieties. I chatted with Masik's CEO, Oren Hexter, and was impressed with his deep, bordering on obsessive, knowledge of olive oil. I asked him if I could visit the farm and photograph a few recipes that make use of their oil, and he agreed to find a chef to work with me. Two weeks later, on a scalding hot spring day, I found myself standing in an olive grove with views of the West Bank, next to a flaming grill, about to photograph the rustic, earthy food created for me by Chef Yohai Nevo.

"The Jewish mind thinks that you can be a chef in a year," Yohai told me, and added as an afterthought, "Everyone is taking life too fast." Yohai is a soulful, introspective man, with a quiet virility that disarms both men and women. After completing his army service, he didn't want to follow in the footsteps of his friends and do drugs in South America, so instead, he hiked through Alaska and Canada, an unusual choice for someone who had just completed a rigorous three years as a soldier. With his post-army hiking behind him, he and a friend created a catering company called Ha'soed Ha'noded—The Wandering Gourmet—and now travel throughout Israel with their grills, throwing dinner parties for which their guests pay a fee to feast on meats, vegetables, and breads, all prepared and cooked on the spot on the grill. While he was stuffing an entire deboned chicken with a mixture of spices, cashews, prunes, and freekeh, a roasted green wheat, I asked him where his recipes came from and he replied, "I take ideas from life."

A few days later, Dorit and I returned to Zichron Ya'acov to try Oratorio, the new restaurant we had stumbled upon on our last photographic expedition. It is nestled in the Elma Arts Complex, a building the Israeli architect Jacob Rechter designed in 1968 to be a sanitarium. The building is shaped like a wave and mimics the curve of the mountain it sits on. Art collector and Zichron native Lily Elstein, whose vision it was to create art galleries, a concert hall, and a luxury hotel, rescued the sanitarium from demolition in 2005 and has made sure ever since that her guests enjoy a dining experience commensurate with such a grand location in the heart of one of Israel's most notable wine regions.

I ordered the Fisherman's Soup because, when it's done properly, there are very few things I enjoy eating more, especially when I am close enough to the sea to inhale a salty breeze. The restaurant's wine cellar was extensive and many local wines were available by the glass, so I felt we were off to an impeccable start. And then the soup arrived. It was flat and tasteless. I told the waiter the soup had no flavor, and no sooner had those words left my mouth than I saw standing before me Ohad Levi, the imposing, curly headed chef. "You're right," he said, "we forgot the seasoning. Let me remake it and I'll send out something else with it." Fair enough I thought. The restaurant had been open for under a month, and good things often come with second chances.

True to his word, everything Chef Levi served in the second wave was delicious, and he turned out to be a personable fellow with a lot of knowledge about the contemporary Israeli food scene. Growing up with a Libyan mother and an Iraqi father instilled in him the idea that Israeli cuisine is an amalgam of flavors from all over the world and an essential part of daily life. He told me, "When you come to someone's house in Israel, they open the refrigerator, put you inside, and you have to eat your way out." It is not an overstatement to say that feeding a friend, a guest, or a new acquaintance is as important to an Israeli host as eating.

Whenever one of my hosts tells me about a person they think I should meet, I listen and I go, even if it means traveling to the other side of the world. Asaf Doktor, a chef in Tel Aviv, told me that Aaron Markovich makes some of the best cheeses in Israel, so one morning during our journey together, Nancy and I drove the agreeably short distance from Tel Aviv to Moshav Nehalim to taste Aaron's cheese.

The instant I saw Aaron waiting for us on the flower-lined path leading to his shop, I liked him. He has a giddy smile, a soft, lined face, and short, sandy gray hair. He was wearing a black muscle T-shirt and a small black kipa; the combined effect evoked a hip and holy sage. After spending the morning with him, I would add crazy to that description, only because he himself kept saying it. He told us he is too demanding and no one will work with him, which suits him fine because he likes to think alone. He is self-taught, has never visited other cheese makers, and believes one cannot go to school to learn his métier. "I don't want to see the *Mona Lisa* and then do the *Mona Lisa*," he explained. There is no doubt that this man follows his heart in everything he does. He told me, "If you put love in, not everybody can do it; if you put in all your heart, nobody can do it."

Aaron creates forty to fifty fresh, ripened, semi-hard, and hard cheese varieties, and uses flowers, rosemary, bay and fig leaves, and wine to add layers of flavor to the sweet and creamy sheep's milk. He loves his thousand sheep and his cheese so much that he wants to know who buys it. He will not sell it unless his customer has tasted it, and he won't allow anyone else to sell it for him. "You don't have to eat much to get the full taste; come hungry and you will leave in love," he rejoiced. Sick people with cancer come for his yogurt because it makes them feel good. He told me, "God gave me a present and I give yogurt back."

Nancy and I both loved the textures and flavors of the cheeses we tasted at Aaron's shop and appreciated the range in the tones of its whiteness. It gave us a pleasing sensation of purity. Aaron's expressive face mirrored our pleasure as he explained that cow's milk is bland and goat's milk is too strong, but sheep's milk falls somewhere in between. He took us into the refrigerated storage room and lifted out a large rack of six big, round cheeses. Each one was covered with edible flowers. "I put exactly one hundred flowers on each cheese," he said. They were the most dazzling cheeses I had ever seen. I asked him what inspired him to make these beautiful cheeses and his answer was "purity."

When Dr. Nof Atamna-Ismaeel, who holds a master's degree in Microbiology and Biotechnology, a PhD in Marine Microbiology, and four postdoctoral degrees, was an exchange student at Ohio University, her nighttime passion was cooking. Her professors told her she was a brilliant scientist but perhaps more importantly, an amazing cook. She would take in her experiment results to discuss with one of her professors, and he would push them aside and ask her what she was having for lunch. She started blogging about food and began to suspect that she had a dual personality. It suddenly dawned on her that the feedback she received about her recipes was instantaneous and gratifying. The idea of people eating and enjoying her food was like a drug. It had always bothered her that when she published a scientific article, only two thousand scientists whom she would never meet would read it.

Nof's eldest son, Raqui, attends an Arabic bilingual school. When she went to the first meeting with the other Jewish and Arab parents, she noticed that the food they all shared broke the obvious tension in the air. Suddenly people were laughing and smiling and sharing recipes; this experience encouraged her to start a bilingual cooking school that could undermine prejudice, something she has struggled with in her own life. She wrote letters to potential donors and agencies for support, but no one responded. When she watched the finale of Israel's *Master Chef* competition and saw Tom Franz win, she thought that if she entered, she could use it as a platform for her cause, so she signed up the next day. " I thought being famous might get people to listen to me. I decided I could use prime time as a platform," she explained. She won first place in the competition and is now a media star and a household name in Israel. She continues to be passionate about her cause and tireless in her efforts to make a change. "I am many things. I don't fit in any box. I'm Israeli, I'm Palestinian, I'm Arab, I'm Muslim, I'm a woman, a mother, and I am enjoying my life as an Israeli but cannot turn my back on my heritage. Is there a point when we will be able to move on?"

During my morning working with Nof, I met her brother, Shadi, who bears a striking resemblance to the American actor Johnny Depp. He is an intelligent, charismatic young dentist who speaks perfect American English with all the requisite slang of a person his age, which he told me he learned from watching American movies. I looked out the window at the views and asked Shadi about Baqa El Garbyya, the village that has been home to his family for generations. He told me that the land I was looking at had belonged to his family before the State of Israel was established. I wondered how this affected him, sixty years later. He turned his gaze from the view, looked at me and said, "Not what was, only what will be. We must use knowledge, not guns. It's more effective." It was enlightening for me to spend the afternoon with this Israeli/Palestinian brother and sister who bantered and laughed together just like my own children do. Shadi urged us to hurry up and finish our shoot so they could go shopping, and to my surprise, I felt completely at home in this normal household just minutes from the West Bank.

Flatbread Stuffed with Fried Onion, Oregano, and Sumac

MAKES 20 TRIANGLES

When I photograph food, I never eat, because if I start, I won't stop. I like to wait until I finish working and then sit down to a civilized meal. When I worked with Amos Sion at Helena, one of his Arab sous chefs prepared these pitas for all of us, and I ate most of them standing up in the kitchen. He served them with a simple dipping sauce of goat's milk yogurt, olive oil, and peeled, chopped tomatoes with minced jalapeños. Try serving these with Jajo's Tomato Salad (page 145).

DOUGH

2½ cups (300 g) bread flour

1¼ cups (300 ml) lukewarm water

2 teaspoons active dry yeast

1 tablespoon olive oil

1 scant tablespoon sea salt

FILLING

¼ cup (60 ml) olive oil

1 large onion, diced

1 cup oregano leaves; reserve
  1 spoonful for garnish

1 tablespoon ground sumac

Salt

3 cups (700 ml) olive oil

FOR DOUGH: Combine all the ingredients in the large bowl of a stand mixer fitted with a bread hook. Mix on low speed until the ingredients are combined and a ball starts to form. Then increase the speed to medium and mix until the dough is smooth and elastic, 10 to 15 minutes. Cover the dough with a damp towel and let rise in a warm, draft-free area until doubled in volume, about 1 hour.

Punch dough down and divide it into 5 balls. Arrange balls on a baking sheet, cover with a towel, and let rise for 30 minutes.

FOR FILLING: Heat the ¼ cup (60 ml) olive oil in a medium-size heavy skillet over medium heat. Add the onion and sauté until soft and golden, about 15 minutes. Stir in the oregano and sumac. Remove from heat and cool completely. Season with salt.

TO ASSEMBLE: Place a ball of dough on a lightly floured surface. Using the heel of one hand, flatten and stretch dough into a rectangle. Lightly dust a rolling pin with flour and roll dough out into a 3 x 8-inch (7.6 x 20 cm) rectangle. Spread a fifth of the filling onto rectangle, then fold into an envelope. Roll dough into 3 x 8-inch (7.6 x 20 cm) rectangle with a ¼ inch (6 mm) thickness. Cut each rectangle in half, then in half again to form 4 triangles. Repeat with remaining dough balls and filling.

TO FRY: Heat the 3 cups olive oil to 375°F (190°C) in a large heavy pot. Add triangles of dough (in batches; do not crowd) and fry until puffed and golden brown, about 3 minutes per side. Remove from oil using a slotted utensil and drain on paper towels. Serve immediately.

Manti with Tomato Salsa and Yogurt

Manti are dumplings that have their origin in Turkish cuisine, and Israel's 2014 Master Chef, Dr. Nof Atamna-Ismaeel, brings them to a new level when she stuffs them with lamb and spices and serves them on a bed of piquant tomato salsa. Chef Nof makes the bold and innovative decision to leave her dumplings open with their tops down, drizzling them with yogurt and sprinkling with sumac—the tart, crimson Middle Eastern spice.

DOUGH

3$\frac{1}{3}$ cups (1 pound; 500 g) all-
    purpose flour
1$\frac{1}{3}$ cups water
Generous $\frac{1}{2}$ tablespoon olive oil
1 teaspoon salt

FILLING

$\frac{1}{4}$ cup olive oil
2 medium onions, finely chopped
1 pound (500 g) ground lamb
1$\frac{1}{2}$ teaspoons baharat
Salt and freshly ground pepper

SALSA

5 ripe plum tomatoes, chopped
$\frac{1}{3}$ cup chopped mint leaves
1 fresh green chili, chopped
2 medium garlic cloves, minced
Juice of $\frac{1}{2}$ lemon
1 tablespoon olive oil
Salt and freshly ground pepper

SERVE

2 cups (17 ounces; 500 ml) whole
    milk yogurt, preferably goat's milk
Ground sumac

FOR DOUGH: Place all the ingredients in the bowl of a stand mixer fitted with a dough hook. Start mixing on low speed until the dough begins to come together. Increase speed to medium and mix until a soft dough forms, about 5 minutes. Cover the dough with a towel and let stand for 15 minutes.

FOR FILLING: Heat the oil in a large heavy skillet over medium heat. Add the onions and sauté until browned but not burned, 10 to 15 minutes. Place the lamb in a large bowl. Add the browned onions and baharat. Season generously with salt and pepper. Using clean hands, blend the meat mixture until it is dough-like, about 5 minutes. Form meat mixture into $\frac{3}{4}$-inch (2 cm) balls; set balls on baking sheets.

TO ASSEMBLE: Preheat the oven to 425°F. Grease a baking sheet or sheets. Turn the dough out onto a floured work surface and cut into 3 equal pieces. Roll each piece out to a minimum thickness of $\frac{1}{8}$ inch (3 mm). Cut each piece into 2-inch (5 cm) squares. Place 1 meatball in the center of each square. Bring all corners of dough into the center over the meatball and pinch together. Arrange the manti on the prepared sheet or sheets. Bake until dough is golden brown and meat is cooked through, about 15 minutes.

FOR SALSA: Place the tomatoes, mint, chili, and garlic in a serving bowl. Squeeze the lemon over everything. Toss with olive oil. Season with salt and pepper.

TO SERVE: Spoon some salsa onto each plate or onto a serving platter. Top with the manti. Dollop with yogurt. Sprinkle with sumac. Serve immediately.

Glazed Burrata with Pumpkin Carpaccio, Pumpkin Seeds, and Fried Sage

Chef Amos Sion served this appetizer to Nancy and me at his restaurant, Helena. The creamy burrata, tender, sweet squash, and crispy pumpkin seeds and sage create a symphony of textures, flavor, and color. Make sure to cut the pumpkin into ultra-thin slices.

7 ounces (200 g) fresh pumpkin, peeled and very thinly sliced, preferably with a mandoline

2 tablespoons powdered sugar

1 teaspoon salt

Juice of 1 lemon

1/4 cup (60 ml) vegetable oil

6 fresh sage leaves

1 ball burrata cheese

1 tablespoon olive oil

2 tablespoons pomegranate molasses or high-quality aged balsamic vinegar

2 tablespoons shelled pumpkin seeds (often sold as pepitas), toasted

Set the pumpkin slices on a baking sheet. Place the powdered sugar in a very small strainer or sieve and dust the pumpkin with an even layer of sugar. Sprinkle evenly with salt. Squeeze the juice of the lemon over it and let it stand until the pumpkin softens slightly, at least 5 minutes, or longer if you prefer softer slices.

Heat the vegetable oil in a small heavy skillet. Fry the sage leaves until they are crisp. Remove from the oil using a slotted utensil and transfer to paper towels.

Line a serving plate with the pumpkin slices. Place the burrata cheese in the center. Drizzle with the olive oil, then the molasses or vinegar. Sprinkle with the pumpkin seeds and fried sage leaves and serve.

Charaima

I am happy to present Smadar Vardi's venerated fish stew. Moroccan paprika is paprika mixed with olive oil and sold in a jar. It is readily available in Middle Eastern markets and by mail order. If you can't find it, mix paprika with a little olive oil before measuring and add it to the dish. Smadar uses whole fish and cuts them into slices, including the head, so the fish is on the bone, which adds a lot of flavor. However, if you prefer fillets, purchase about four pounds of whatever firm-fleshed fish you like, cut them into chunks, and then add them to the marinade. Don't forget to put a few whole challahs on the table so your guests can tear off generous hunks for mopping up the sauce.

FISH

1 cup (16 g) fresh cilantro leaves
1/2 cup (120 ml) fresh lemon juice
1/4 cup (60 ml) olive oil
1 tablespoon Moroccan paprika
1 teaspoon ground white pepper
1 teaspoon salt
5 pounds (2.26 kg) grouper, mahi mahi, or sea bass, cut into 2-inch-thick (5 cm) slices (including head and bones)

SAUCE

1/4 cup (60 ml) olive oil
10 garlic cloves, peeled
3 dried sweet red chilies
3 fresh long green spicy chilies
2 dried spicy red chilies
2 tablespoons Moroccan paprika
2 teaspoons ground cumin
2 teaspoons salt
1 teaspoon smoked paprika
1 teaspoon ground white pepper
1 teaspoon crushed fennel seed
8 cups (1.9 l) cold water
Chopped fresh cilantro

FOR FISH: Combine the first 6 ingredients in large bowl. Add the fish pieces and submerge them in the marinade. Let stand for 30 minutes.

FOR SAUCE: Heat the oil in a large heavy skillet over medium heat. Add the garlic cloves and sauté until lightly browned. Add the next 9 ingredients and sauté for 2 minutes. Add the water, cover, and simmer for 30 minutes. Uncover and simmer for 10 minutes. Add the fish with its marinade to the skillet and simmer until fish is cooked through, about 15 minutes, adjusting heat if necessary to maintain a gentle simmer. Remove from heat, cover, and let stand for 10 minutes before serving. Adjust the seasoning with salt. Garnish with chopped cilantro and serve with challah.

Matfune

The bursts of flavor in Yohai Nevo's coal-roasted boneless chicken stuffed with spiced freekeh, prunes, and cashews are extraordinary. Freekeh is a roasted young green wheat with a subtle smoky flavor and chewy texture. It needs to be soaked for five hours, so make sure to plan ahead. You may substitute bulgur wheat if freekeh isn't available. If the idea of coal roasting is alarming, get over it. Once you try it, you'll be throwing everything on the coals; but if you wish, this chicken can be cooked on the grill or in the oven. If you've never boned a chicken and lack the confidence to try doing it yourself, ask your butcher to do it for you.

STUFFING

1½ cups (8 to 9 ounces; 250 g) freekeh

½ cup (3.5 ounces; 70 g) chopped pitted prunes

½ cup (3.5 ounces; 70 g) roasted cashews, salted if desired

⅓ cup (80 ml) extra virgin olive oil

1 tablespoon sumac

1 tablespoon honey

1 teaspoon salt

1 teaspoon ground turmeric

1 teaspoon ground cumin

½ teaspoon freshly ground pepper

¼ teaspoon ground allspice

CHICKEN

1 large whole chicken, boned

2 tablespoons olive oil

2 teaspoons salt

1 teaspoon freshly ground black pepper

1 tablespoon ground cumin

1 teaspoon sweet paprika

1 teaspoon sugar

FOR STUFFING: Place the freekeh in a large bowl. Cover it with water and let stand for 5 hours. Drain freekeh and wipe out the bowl. Return freekeh to the bowl, add all remaining stuffing ingredients, and mix well.

FOR CHICKEN: Lay the chicken skin-side up on a cutting board. Rub it with olive oil. Season with salt and pepper. Sprinkle with cumin, paprika, and sugar. Turn chicken over. Mound the stuffing in the center of the chicken (any leftover stuffing is delicious on its own). Bring the sides of the chicken up around the filling to form a ball. Wrap in 3 layers of aluminum foil and seal well.

Prepare the coals and preheat the grill to high, or the oven to its highest setting. Set the foil packet directly on the coals or grill (if using a grill, cover it with a lid) and cook for 15 minutes. Turn packet over and cook for an additional 15 minutes. Set grill about 4 inches (10 cm) over the coals and continue cooking for 30 minutes, turning once halfway through. (If cooking on a grill or in the oven, just continue cooking for 30 minutes.) Let chicken stand in the foil for 10 minutes. Unwrap chicken, cut into slices, and serve.

Gondolas

Eran Borkin told me the inspiration for this recipe is a fusion of two things he loves: the Hachipouri from Georgia—a bread with an egg inside—and a Turkish bread stuffed with scrambled eggs and cheese. His version is unique because he builds the edges of the crust up by stuffing them with cherry tomatoes and cheese. Make sure to start the dough for this recipe twenty-four hours before you plan to prepare it.

DOUGH

4½ cups (560 g) all-purpose flour

½ cup (65 g) rye flour

1 tablespoon salt

1 tablespoon instant dry yeast

3 cups (700 ml) very cold water

½ cup (120 ml) olive oil

HERB BUTTER

7 tablespoons butter, room
   temperature

2 cups chopped fresh herbs

1 tablespoon Dijon mustard

1 medium garlic clove, crushed

Salt and freshly ground pepper

CHEESE FILLING

1 cup (250 g) whole milk ricotta
   cheese

1 cup (150 g) crumbled feta cheese

1 cup (110 g) shredded mozzarella
   cheese

Salt and freshly ground pepper

ASSEMBLY

All-purpose flour

1 pint (320 g) cherry tomatoes,
   halved

8 eggs

½ cup (55 g) shredded mozzarella

FOR DOUGH: Place both flours, salt, and yeast in the bowl of a stand mixer fitted with a dough hook. Mix to combine. Gradually add the water and mix on low speed for 7 minutes. Increase speed to 4 and beat until the dough starts to come together, about 4 minutes. Gradually beat in the oil on the same speed and mix until dough is velvety and does not stick to the sides of the bowl, about 5 minutes. Turn dough out onto a work surface and cut the dough into 4 pieces. Place each piece in a separate oiled ziplock bag and refrigerate for 24 hours.

FOR BUTTER: Place the first 4 ingredients in a food processor and blend until combined. Turn the butter mixture into a bowl. Season with salt and pepper. Let stand at room temperature until ready to use, or wrap in plastic and refrigerate or freeze until ready to use.

FOR FILLING: Place all of the cheeses in a bowl and mix well using a wooden spoon. Season with salt and pepper.

TO ASSEMBLE: Preheat the oven to 450 to 500°F (230 to 260°C). Heavily flour a work surface. Roll out each ball of dough into a 7- to 8-inch (18 to 20 cm) round. Arrange a few cherry tomato halves around the edge of the first dough round, leaving space in between. Spoon a bit of the cheese filling in between tomato halves. Fold the dough edge over to cover tomatoes and cheese and to form a gondola shape; press and crimp to seal. Spread 1 tablespoon herb butter in the center of the dough. Break 2 eggs atop butter. Sprinkle with some shredded mozzarella. Repeat to make 3 more gondolas. Arrange gondolas on a baking sheet. Bake until the crust is cooked through and golden brown and the eggs are cooked, 15 to 20 minutes. Serve immediately.

Vanilla Ice Cream with Cherry Tomato Jam

Here is an inventive dessert from retired F-14-pilot-turned-chef Benny Ben Israel. The combination of cherry tomatoes and ice cream might be a stretch for some, but it is truly an excellent and surprisingly tasty marriage. The crunchy and spicy black peppercorns are a nice contrast to the sweetness of the other ingredients.

1 pound (450 g) cherry tomatoes

1²/₃ (330 g) cups sugar

2 tablespoons water

1 tablespoon black peppercorns

2 pints (1 l) best-quality vanilla ice cream

Chopped fresh mint leaves

Combine the tomatoes, sugar, water, and peppercorns in a medium-size heavy pot and bring to a boil. Reduce the heat and simmer, stirring occasionally, until the mixture is thick, syrupy, and reduced by half, about 1 hour. Cool completely, then refrigerate until ready to use.

Divide the ice cream among bowls or coupes. Spoon the tomato jam over the ice cream. Garnish with mint and serve immediately.

Coal-Roasted Vegetables with Honey and Celery Leaves

8 SERVINGS

The idea of roasting these earthy vegetables right on the coals is genius but not recommended for the faint of heart who are in a rush to eat. Yohai Nevo prepares this with casual confidence, and when he opened up the foil and a cloud of fragrant steam emerged, we all swooned. If you can't use Masik's excellent olive oil, use the best you can find. It makes a big difference.

2 fennel bulbs, trimmed of hard outer leaves, cut into 1-inch (2.5 cm) cubes (about 3 cups)

2 beets, unpeeled, cut into $1/4$-inch (6 mm) cubes (about $1^1/2$ cups)

1 sweet potato, unpeeled, cut into 1-inch (2.5 cm) cubes (about $2^1/4$ cups)

1 kohlrabi, peeled, cut into 1-inch (2.5 cm) cubes (about 1 cup)

1 large zucchini, cut into 1-inch (2.5 cm) cubes (about 2 cups)

$1/2$ large lemon, thinly sliced

5 large garlic cloves, crushed

$1/3$ cup (80 ml) extra virgin olive oil

$1/4$ cup (60 g) chopped fresh celery leaves

2 tablespoons honey

$1^1/2$ tablespoons salt

$1/2$ teaspoon freshly ground pepper

Prepare the coals, preheat the grill, or preheat the oven to 450°F (230°C).

Place all ingredients in a large bowl and mix well. Transfer the mixture to 3 layers of aluminum foil and seal well if cooking in coals or on a grill, or transfer to a baking sheet or pan if cooking in the oven. Place the foil packet directly on the coals or grill and cook for 25 minutes on each side; or roast in the oven for 30 minutes, then shake the pan or stir the vegetables and continue roasting until the vegetables are evenly caramelized, 15 to 20 minutes. Adjust the seasoning with salt and pepper if desired. Serve immediately with Chicken and Mushroom Roulade (page 152).

OVERLEAF: AARON MARKOVICH'S ONE HUNDRED FLOWER SHEEP CHEESES.

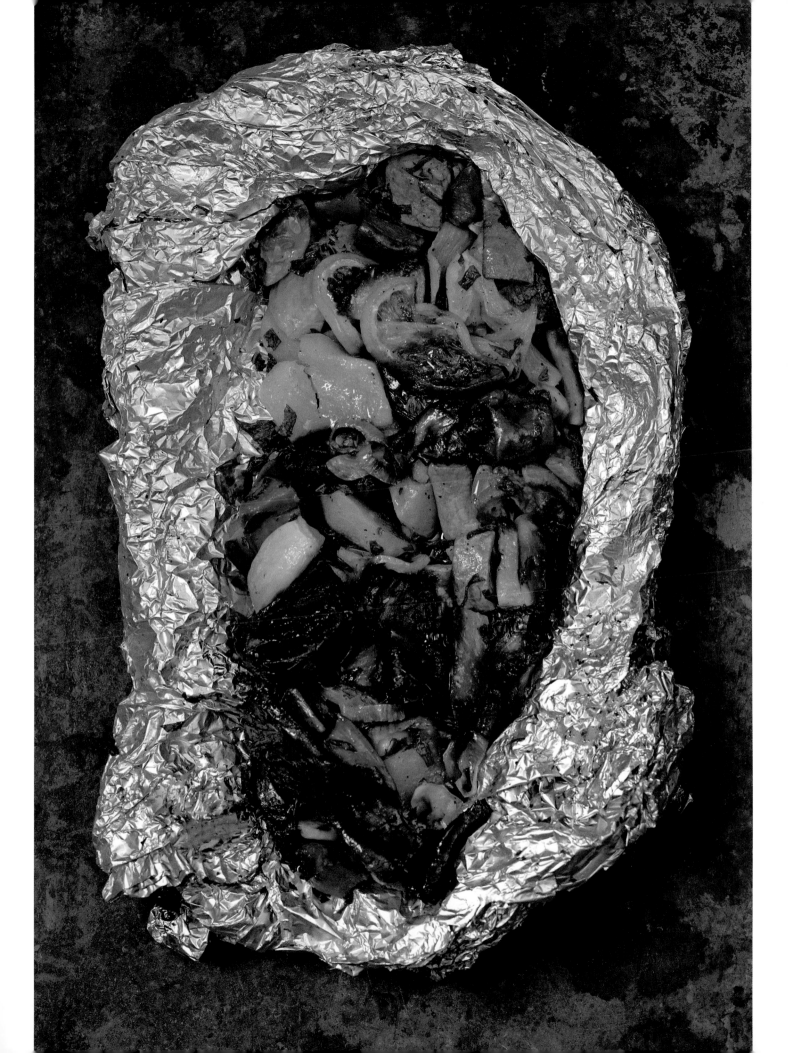

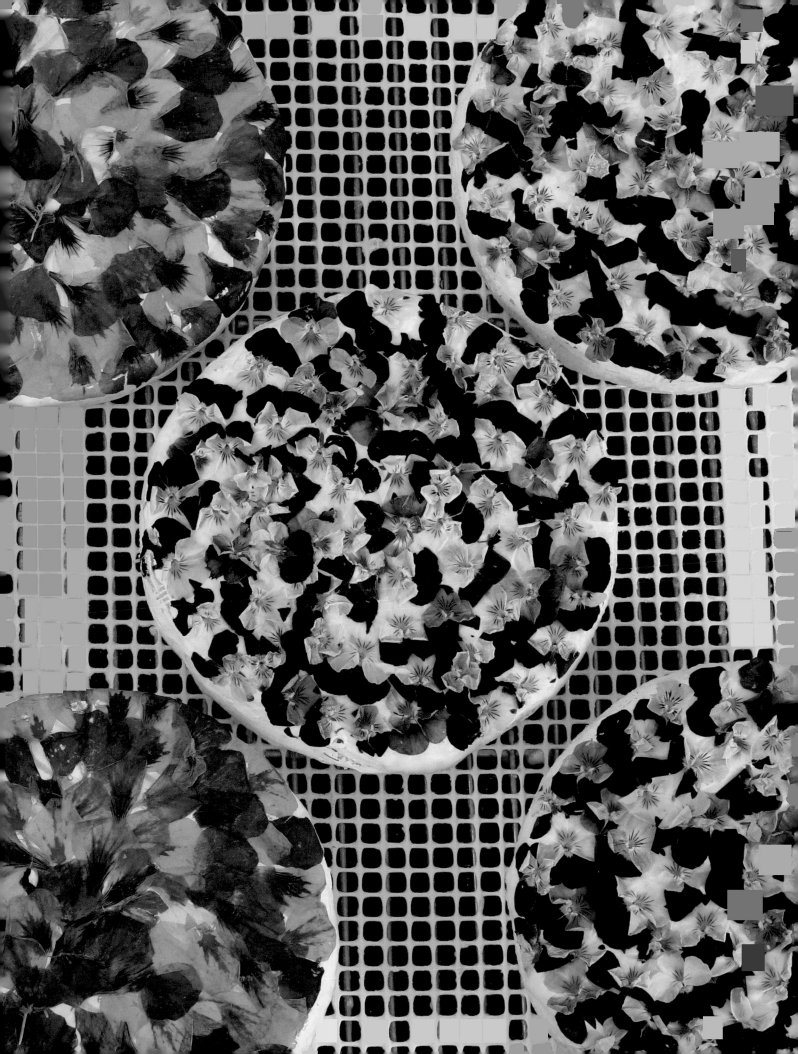

Stuffed Cabbage Cake

When I arrived at Oratorio in Zichron Ya'acov the day of the shoot, Chef Ohad Levi proudly presented this to me on a platter as if it were a rare wild mushroom that he had unearthed in the woods. It was beautiful in its organic roundness and I was very inspired. His stuffing is a fragrant mixture of rice, lamb, onion, dried cranberries, pine nuts, mint, tomatoes, and the Middle Eastern spice mixture *ras el hanout*. Make sure to start the dish two days before you plan to serve it; you need one day for freezing the cabbage and one day for refrigerating the finished dish.

1 medium green cabbage

1 cup (190 g) jasmine rice, rinsed

5 tablespoons olive oil, divided

1 small onion, minced

21 ounces (600 g) ground lamb

½ cup (20 g) chopped mint leaves

2 medium tomatoes, grated

2 tablespoons toasted pine nuts

2 tablespoons chopped dried
  cranberries

1 teaspoon ras el hanout

Salt and freshly ground pepper

1 generous cup (200 ml) chicken
  stock or broth

⅓ cup (80 ml) fresh lemon juice

1 large garlic clove, crushed

Freeze the cabbage for 24 hours to facilitate separating of leaves.

Defrost the cabbage. Separate leaves, trying not to rip them. The more whole leaves, the better.

Bring a small pot of water to a boil. Add the rice and simmer for 20 minutes. Drain.

Heat 2 tablespoons of the olive oil in a large heavy skillet over medium heat. Add the onion and sauté until softened, about 5 minutes. Add the lamb and sauté until browned and no pink remains, 8 to 10 minutes. Stir in the blanched rice, mint, tomatoes, pine nuts, cranberries, and ras el hanout. Season generously with salt and pepper.

Preheat the oven to 350°F (175°C). Arrange one-fourth of the cabbage leaves in the bottom of a medium-size Dutch oven or heavy pot. Top with a third of the meat mixture. Cover with another fourth of the cabbage leaves. Top with another third of the meat mixture. Cover with another fourth of the cabbage leaves. Top with the remaining third of the meat mixture. Cover with the remaining fourth of the cabbage leaves. Pour in the chicken stock and lemon juice. Add the garlic clove and season generously with salt and pepper. Cover tightly and cook for 1½ hours.

Remove the lid from the pot. Cover contents of the pot with a plate, then top the plate with a brick or cans as weight. Refrigerate overnight.

Bring the cabbage cake to room temperature. Cut it into slices to serve.

Tel-Aviv Style Ashkenazi Knafeh

This wild riff on *knafeh* illustrates Benny Ben Israel's belief that Israelis are in the vanguard of culinary creativity. He has taken the classic Middle Eastern dessert and updated it with modern ingredients. On top of shredded *kadaif* pastry, he puts mascarpone cheese and Grand Marnier crème, candied beets and beet syrup, and a salty toffee sauce to finish it off. I was skeptical when he threw this together until I put the first big spoonful in my mouth.

BASE

10½ ounces (300 g) kadaif pastry
(shredded phyllo pastry)

½ cup (1 stick; 4 ounces; 113 g)
butter, melted

CANDIED BEETS

2 small beets or 1 medium-to-large
beet, peeled and cut into ¼-inch
(6 mm) cubes

1 cup (240 ml) water

½ cup (100) sugar

3 star anise pods

SALTY TOFFEE SAUCE

1 generous cup (250 ml) heavy
cream

2 teaspoons salt

1 cup (200 g) sugar

⅔ scant cup (150 ml) crème
fraîche

FOR BASE: Preheat the oven to 350°F (175°C). Gently unfold the kadaif and fluff out. Pour the butter into a bowl. Add the kadaif and submerge it, then toss to distribute butter as evenly as possible. Transfer to a baking sheet and divide it into 6 portions, mounding each gently. Bake until golden brown, about 15 minutes. Cool completely.

FOR BEETS: Combine the beet cubes, water, sugar, and star anise in a medium-size heavy saucepan and bring to a boil. Reduce heat and simmer until beet cubes are fork-tender but not mushy, 20 to 30 minutes. Using a slotted utensil, transfer beet cubes from the pan to a plate and cool completely. Continue simmering the cooking liquid until it is thick in texture, about 7 minutes. Cool completely.

FOR TOFFEE: Combine the cream and salt in a small heavy saucepan over medium heat and heat until bubbles start to form around the edges of the pan; do not boil. Place the sugar in another small heavy saucepan over medium-low heat. When sugar starts to liquefy, start swirling it around in the pan. When most of the sugar is melted and starting to brown, stir with a rubber spatula. Continue cooking until a golden brown caramel forms. Off of the heat, vigorously stir the heated cream into the caramelized sugar (stand back; the mixture might bubble), then stir the crème fraîche into the mixture.

GRAND MARNIER CREAM

1 cup (250 g) mascarpone

3 tablespoons Grand Marnier or other orange-flavored liqueur

1 generous cup (250 ml) heavy cream

¾ cup (100 g) powdered sugar

ASSEMBLY

1 cup (3½ ounces; 100 g) sliced almonds, toasted

FOR CREAM: Place the mascarpone and liqueur in a bowl and whisk until it is the texture of thick yogurt. Place the cream and sugar in another bowl and beat with a whisk or electric mixer until thick. Fold both creams together and transfer mixture to a piping bag fitted with a star tip.

FOR ASSEMBLY: Spread a thin layer of beet syrup on each of 6 dessert plates. Top each with a mound of kadaif. Pipe a layer of cream over the kadaif. Drizzle it with toffee sauce and decorate it with beet cubes. Garnish with almonds and serve immediately.

Tahini Cookies

Dorit brought these cookies home from one of her shopping forays and when I tasted them, I had to meet the person who made them. I found light green–eyed Ella Boimel Goren in her lovely light-filled bakery, Patisserie Ella, when I was on the way to the airport. She generously wrote down this recipe for me, let me photograph the cookies, and gave me a sandwich and more cookies for my journey. She told me that when she was pregnant with her daughter Gily (which means "my happiness"), she had been on bed rest for six months. After crying for three weeks, she wondered, "What am I going to do with myself?" and decided to teach herself how to bake. She sat on her sofa with her big belly, not allowed to move, and mixed bread dough every day, testing recipes.

2 sticks (1 cup; 230 g) butter, room temperature

1 cup (200 g) sugar

1 cup (240 g) absolute best-quality tahini

3 cups (375 g) all-purpose flour

2 teaspoons baking powder

Place the butter and sugar in the large bowl of a stand mixer. Cream butter and sugar until light and fluffy. Beat in the tahini. Add the flour and baking powder and beat to combine. Let the dough stand for 1 hour.

Position the rack in the center of the oven and preheat oven to 350°F (175°C). Form dough into scant 1½-inch (3.8 cm) rounds. Arrange rounds on baking sheets (do not crowd) and bake until slightly brown, about 20 minutes. Let the cookies cool for 2 to 3 minutes on baking sheets. Transfer to a cooling rack to cool completely. Store in an airtight container.

Sweet Potatoes with Crème Fraîche, Feta, and Dill

This is quite simply one of the best ways to eat a yam. Benny Ben Israel is a gifted innovator who can feed the soul with the simplest, freshest ingredients. I enjoy eating these sweet potatoes without accompaniment because I don't want anything to distract from the perfect harmony of the exquisite flavors. Make sure each and every ingredient is of the highest quality.

4 pounds (1.8 kg) salt

10 small sweet potatoes, washed but not peeled

1 cup (8 ounces; 240 ml) crème fraîche

8 ounces (150 g) feta cheese, crumbled

⅓ cup (13 g) chopped fresh dill

Preheat the oven to 425°F (220°C). Place the salt on a baking sheet. Nestle the sweet potatoes in the salt so they are covered up halfway. Bake until potatoes are completely cooked through, about 40 minutes.

Arrange the sweet potatoes on a serving platter. Cut open each potato halfway. Spoon some crème fraîche into each potato. Sprinkle with feta and garnish with dill. Serve immediately.

of dogs howled. It was a primal sound that entered into the spot between my heart and the pit of my stomach. And then I heard and felt the roar of aircraft engines above my head. I worried about another war, about being prevented from finishing my work, and about how a situation that I could not control could impact my life and affect the choices I made. And I was a visitor here. I could pack my bags, get on a plane, and return to my tranquil existence in Napa Valley. What if my family and my work were here and I lived with this frightening uncertainty every day of my life? The barking was constant until the birds took over at dawn. I put on Debussy and wondered if it was just my imagination, or if everything felt a little surreal, like a bright and fresh veneer on the fears of the dark night.

Yaara and I finished our work together—no more rockets were fired, no visits to the bomb shelter were required; then I left to explore the Arava, the swath of desert that shares the border with Jordan and stretches from the Dead to the Red Seas. On a lonesome stretch of road, I passed a sign for a café called Ursula. I made a U-turn to go back and see who Ursula was and what she served.

I walked in the door, leaving the hot, dry air outside, with my camera and long telephoto lens slung over my shoulder. A woman sitting at the bar eating a sausage called out to me and asked if I photographed birds. I said no, food, and the man behind the bar told me to sit down and have a glass of water and something to eat. Judy Garland was singing "Over the Rainbow" as the woman leaned toward me and said, "Don't you love this music?" The previous night I had been worrying about war and bombs and comparing my experience to a Disney film, and this afternoon I was in a café chatting about The Wizard of Oz with strangers. This is the paradox of Israel.

The sausage-eating woman turned out to be German-born Ursula Winter, a holistic healer who, while conducting a geological field study in southern Israel, had also led Israel soldiers on guided tours of the area. When she finished her field study, she had stopped giving the tours as well and had no real plans for her immediate future. There had been no obvious source of income in the Arava, but she had an idea. She would open a café on the road from the north to Eilat, sell local products, and serve food to the travelers on their long journey south. She had asked herself what she could do that was different, and the answer she had come up with was "serve German food!" Ursula's café is homey, with wood tables and chairs and brightly colored checked place mats; the menu ranges from a light bowl of baby zucchini soup with mint and lemon to hearty plates of knockwurst with sauerkraut and potatoes.

Ursula and I talked about the cuisine in the south, and I mentioned that I had been to the famous restaurant in Eilat and had eaten an awful meal. She told me that it was the first restaurant in the south to offer non-kosher seafood and that the menu had not changed in twenty years. Was it possible to find a better meal around here, I asked?

Within minutes, I was in a golf cart on my way to visit Eretz Arava, a hotel and restaurant in Zuqim. My escort was its manager, Aviad, and when I saw the sand-colored stucco building rising up out of the desert against the majestic backdrop of the marbled hills, I asked him if there was a room available for the night. He told me that Eretz Arava books up weeks, even months in advance; when I asked if everyone had arrived for the night and wondered aloud if it wasn't remotely possible that there might be a last-minute cancellation, he scoffed and said it was highly unlikely.

We sat together, drank a coffee, and talked. Israelis don't shy away from revealing themselves or discussing difficult subjects. In my conversation with this man I had just met, I began to realize that

Broccoli Pie

There were two important issues to consider when I asked Yaara Nir Kachlon to share a few of her recipes with me. The first was that whatever Yaara prepared for me to shoot that day must also be lunch for her husband, Guy, and their four children, and the other was that it would showcase one of her beautiful handmade dishes. She is a gifted ceramic artist who generously loaned me a few of her pieces to use in my photographs. I think this savory pie resolves all of our concerns and looks especially appetizing with the two eggplant blossoms from Guy's nearby farm on the Moshav Klachim.

1¹/₄ (600 g) broccoli, divided into florets

¹/₄ cup (60 g) (¹/₂ stick) butter

3 tablespoons all-purpose flour

1 tablespoon mustard seeds

1 cup (240 ml) whole milk

Salt and freshly ground pepper

1 (8-ounce) package cream cheese (230 grams), cut into small pieces, room temperature

1 cup (230 g) sour cream

3 tablespoons mayonnaise

3 eggs, room temperature, beaten to blend

OVERLEAF: MUSICIAN ORI TOLEDANO AND DALIT AT THE DEAD SEA.

Preheat oven to 350°F (175°C). Grease a 9 x 13-inch (23 x 32.5 cm) baking dish. Bring a large pot of salted water to a boil. Add the broccoli florets and boil until fork-tender, about 4 minutes. Drain and rinse under cold water.

Melt the butter in a medium-size heavy saucepan over medium heat. Add the flour and mustard seeds and whisk for 1 minute. Whisk in the milk. Increase heat and bring to boil, whisking occasionally. Reduce heat and simmer until the sauce thickens, whisking constantly, about 5 minutes. Season sauce with salt and pepper.

Place cream cheese, sour cream, and mayonnaise in a large bowl and mix well. Stir in the eggs. Stir in the sauce. Gently fold in broccoli florets. Season with salt and pepper. Transfer to prepared pan. Bake until just golden brown on top, about 30 minutes. Cut into pieces and serve.

Hagar in the Oven

The golden afternoon light spilled across a landscape that was still dotted with the ruins of a farm from the Middle Bronze period as I savored this rustic and hearty potato and Camembert cheese gratin at the Kornmehl Farm in the Negev Highland. Daniel and Anat Kornmehl created this delicious combination to serve in the restaurant on their farm in honor of their prized goat, Hagar, and I wondered if the people who stood in this very spot 5,000 years ago had ever tasted anything quite this delicious.

1 cup (254 g) whole milk yogurt, preferably goat's milk

2 medium garlic cloves, crushed

$1/4$ teaspoon sea salt

$1/4$ teaspoon freshly ground pepper

2 large red-skinned boiling potatoes

Olive oil

1 whole ripe Camembert cheese (about 9 ounces; 250 grams), room temperature

Combine the yogurt, garlic, salt and pepper in small bowl. Let yogurt sauce stand until ready to use.

Boil or steam the potatoes until tender.

Preheat the broiler. Transfer potatoes to a baking sheet or pan. Broil potatoes until charred on all sides. Cool potatoes, then cut into thin slices.

Drizzle olive oil on two ovenproof plates or individual gratin pans or baking dishes. Arrange potatoes slices atop the olive oil. Cut Camembert crosswise in half. Then cut each half laterally so it opens like a book. Lay each opened cheese half cheese-side up and rind-side down atop sliced potatoes. (Alternatively, remove rind from cheese. Cut cheese into chunks. Dot potatoes with cheese chunks.) Broil until the cheese melts over the potatoes. Serve immediately with yogurt sauce.

Edna Sticks with Sweet Wine Apple Sauce

Many of my reliable sources confirmed that Anat and Daniel Kornmehl make some of the best artisanal goat cheeses in Israel. They own and operate Kornmehl Farm in the Negev Highland and name the cheese dishes they serve in their open-air restaurant after their favorite goats. This confection, a chewy whole-wheat pastry stuffed with soft tangy Gouda and doused in a fragrant fresh apple syrup, pays homage to Edna, a lady who, I was told, never bleated a mean thing in her life.

APPLE SYRUP

2 large apples, peeled, cored, and
   coarsely chopped
1 (750 ml; approximately 27-ounce)
   bottle dry red wine
2 cups (400 g) sugar
Peel of 1 lemon
1 cinnamon stick
2 cloves

DOUGH

$1^1/_2$ cups (190 g) all-purpose flour
1 cup (120 g) whole-wheat flour
$^3/_4$ cup (180 g) whole milk yogurt,
   preferably goat's milk
$^1/_3$ cup (70 g) sugar
2 generous teaspoons active dry
   yeast
Pinch of salt
2 tablespoons water (if needed)
14 tablespoons ($1^3/_4$ sticks; 200 g)
   butter, room temperature

ASSEMBLY

All-purpose flour
10 ounces (280 g) Gouda cheese,
   preferably goat's milk, shredded

APPLE SYRUP: Combine all ingredients in a medium-size, nonreactive, heavy saucepan and bring to a boil. Reduce the heat and simmer until the liquid is thick and syrupy, swirling the pan occasionally, for about 1 hour. Strain the liquid into another large, nonreactive, heavy saucepan and discard the solids. Continue simmering the strained liquid to reduce it even further if desired.

FOR DOUGH: Combine both flours and the yogurt, sugar, yeast, and salt in the bowl of a stand mixer fitted with a dough hook. Mix on low speed until dough starts to pull away from sides of the bowl. Increase the speed to medium and mix until dough starts to come together, adding up to 2 tablespoons water if the mixture is too dry. Add the butter and continue mixing on medium until the dough forms a soft ball, then continue mixing for 5 more minutes. Place dough into an oiled bowl. Cover with plastic wrap and refrigerate for 2 hours.

FOR ASSEMBLY: Preheat oven to 400°F (200°C). Line a baking sheet or sheets with parchment paper. Lightly flour your work surface, rolling pin, and/or hands. Roll or shape the dough into a log. Cut log into 10 pieces. Roll each dough piece out into a 5-inch (13 cm) round. Place $2^1/_2$ tablespoons of the grated cheese into the center of each round. Fold the dough over the cheese, carefully pressing the area close to the filling to eliminate any air pockets. Crimp the outer edges to seal. Arrange on prepared sheets and bake until golden brown, 10 to 15 minutes.

TO SERVE: Set 1 pastry on each plate. Drizzle with apple syrup.

Old City Lemonade

Lemonade is a highly subjective concept. Everyone I know who drinks it has a different opinion of how sweet or how sour it should be. When I arrived at Gan Yarak one sweltering afternoon, Ronit and Moti Elazari immediately put a chilled glass of their tangy lemonade into my soggy hand, and it was better than anything I had ever tasted. Their secret? Puréeing the liquid with the skin of one of the lemons and then straining it out. They told me this technique is from the Old City in Jerusalem, where people crave strong tastes. The Meyer lemons give it a beautiful milky, opaque quality, but if you appreciate extreme bitterness, use regular lemons. If you prefer your lemonade sweeter, add more honey or use sugar or fresh Stevia leaves. It will be most satisfying when you fine-tune the technique to your own expectations of what a good glass of lemonade is.

2 Meyer Lemons

4 cups (1 liter) spring water

2 tablespoons organic honey

Juice one of the lemons, discard the skin, and cut the other lemon into eighths and remove its seeds.

Pour the water into a blender and add the lemon juice, lemon pieces, and honey. (As a refreshing option, peel and roughly chop a hunk of fresh ginger and blend with the other ingredients.)

Blend on the highest speed until the lemon pieces are completely puréed.

Strain the liquid into a pitcher and discard the puréed lemon peel and skin.

Chill the lemonade until ready to serve, about 2 hours.

To serve, pour the lemonade into glasses over ice and garnish with fresh mint, lemon grass, or lemon verbena.

French master pastry chef Pierre Hermé, a refreshing watermelon and tomato gazpacho, or a salad accompanied by quinoa patties suggest a refined home-style cooking that will nourish hungry wanderers and natives alike who seek a modern European spin on Middle Eastern classics.

The Old City Market spills into four distinct quarters—Muslim, Jewish, Christian, and Armenian—and is a wholly different experience from the Mahane Yehuda Market. When you wade through the tourist shops and reach the heart of the market, you come upon a distilled, exotic atmosphere that can be addictive. I find that whenever I am in Jerusalem, the narrow, circuitous paths of the Old City Market pull me deeper and deeper into what feels like a lost world.

In the heart of the Muslim quarter, I stopped in front of an eight-by-ten-foot restaurant dining room where a young man stood at a counter in front of a tall metal vessel that had an opening just large enough for him to reach in and scoop out an appetizing helping of hummus onto small plastic plates. The place had no sign and the few tables in the room had been commandeered by a group of stern-looking men, a few of them wearing the traditional Arab *keffiyeh* on their heads. The aroma of the place was enticing and I made the snap decision to sit down, share a table, and eat. Two men faced me and avoided my eyes. At the next table, a boisterous diner cleared his throat with gusto and loudly spit into his napkin. My dining companions looked at him, then at each other, and turned back to glare at our ill-mannered neighbor. I tried to catch their eyes to commiserate with them, but they were not interested in my point of view. A young boy brought us each a small round bowl with a layer of oil at the bottom and on the top, a layer of hummus garnished with chickpeas and a generous smear of *ful*, the delectable fava bean stew, and a small oval plate of perfectly pickled and seasoned cucumbers and hot green peppers. The boy tore off a piece of paper towel from a roll hanging on the wall, reached into a wooden box covered with cloth, and pulled out six steaming pita breads, which he wrapped in the paper and tossed onto the table. They were soft and doughy, lightly dusted with flour, and the perfect foil for the slippery smooth, well-balanced hummus topped with the smoky *ful*. I was happy dining with these unfriendly strangers and whether they knew it or not, we were enjoying this simple and satisfying meal together.

On another visit to the market, Nancy and I were accompanied by Tomer Niv, the chef at Rama's Kitchen in Nataf, a restaurant in the Judean Hills fifteen minutes from Jerusalem. Tomer is an intense and cerebral man with an unwavering dedication to his philosophy of bringing out the essential characters of each ingredient. He is also a renegade who searches for original ideas using local products that would only have been available on the Silk Road, the 4,000-mile trade route than ran from east to west until the fifteenth century. As Tomer explained it to me during our visit, "This terroir is not Israeli, it is the Middle Eastern region; natural products don't know borders . . . this is planet Earth, I'm here, and I don't care about Israel when I'm cooking." Tomer's indifference to the inescapable political strife surrounding him is also reflected in how he runs his restaurant. "All my cooks are Muslim," he explained. "They leave their backgrounds out of the kitchen to be serious." His choice to deconstruct ethnic boundaries and have Muslims and Jews working together in his restaurant was a decision I respected.

The fruits and vegetables Tomer uses are organic and mostly homegrown, and the herbs are either wild or from the nursery that surrounds the restaurant. Rows of flowering plants and herbs are a visitor's first sight upon their arrival. Tomer likes to cook his ingredients in broths made from their own skins and peelings, like his cauliflower soup, which uses the vegetable's stem and leaves to flavor the broth.

PREVIOUS OVERLEAF: VIEW FROM THE TOWER OF DAVID. FACING: THE SONG OF THE ASCENT WRITTEN ON THE WALL OF A VEGETABLE STAND IN THE MAHANE YEHUDA MARKET.

Fresh Fig, Arugula, and Cheese Salad with Honey Lemon Dressing

The visual beauty of this salad, which is equal to its marvelous flavor, lies in the contrast between the hand-torn and sliced pieces of fig. Majda's Chef Jalil Jalil uses only the freshest, most pungent wild arugula to compete with the sweet figs and honey lemon dressing.

1/2 cup (120 ml) honey

1/2 cup (120 ml) fresh lemon juice

8 fresh figs, sliced

8 fresh figs, hand-torn into four pieces

6 ounces (170 g) arugula

1/2 pound (230 g) feta cheese, crumbled

4 tablespoons extra virgin olive oil

Sea salt

Place the honey and lemon juice in a small heavy saucepan. Bring to a boil, stirring occasionally. Remove from the heat and let the dressing cool to room temperature.

Arrange 2 sliced figs and 2 quartered figs on each of 4 salad plates. Divide arugula among the plates and scatter over figs. Divide cheese among plates. Spoon dressing over salad to taste; you may have some left over. Drizzle 1 tablespoon oil over each plate. Season with sea salt and serve.

PREVIOUS OVERLEAF: CHEF MOSHE BASSON UNDER A CAROB TREE IN THE LAND OF THE MACABEES.

Nancy's Falafel Pistachios

Before I left for my trip to Israel with Steven, I had a meeting with the California Pistachio Board. They were planning a lunch at my restaurant Chi Spacca to showcase recipes I was developing that highlighted pistachios. I told them I would soon be on my way to Israel and would return with at least one Israeli recipe to add to the mix because I knew that the pistachio was the peanut of not only Israel but the entire Middle East. Indeed, pistachios were sold at nearly every market I visited in Israel and were widely deployed—and enjoyed—in many dishes. This particular recipe was inspired by the falafel I ate at the wonderful Arab market in Akko. It was so striking that after asking the falafel man what spices were involved, I went to the spice guy at the same market and requested that he re-create the blend. I was a bit concerned that he would not be able to duplicate the mix. But it turned out that my request was not unique. He quickly began grinding away as if he had done this a thousand times. My request was merely the one thousand first.

1 tablespoon ground cumin

1 tablespoon ground coriander

1 tablespoon dried ground basil

1 tablespoon dried ground
   marjoram

1 tablespoon dried ground
   rosemary

2$^1/_2$ teaspoon turmeric

2 cups (300 g) whole peeled garlic
   cloves

2 cups (475 ml) olive oil

6 dried hot red chilies, such as
   chilies de arbol or pequin chilies

4 cups (500 g) unsalted pistachios
   in the shell

1 teaspoon salt

Combine the first 6 ingredients in a small bowl. Set aside the "falafel" spice.

Line a plate with paper towels. Using a mandolin with a safety attachment to protect your fingers, cut the garlic cloves into paper-thin slices. Pour olive oil into a medium-size heavy skillet and heat over medium-high heat. Add the garlic slices and cook until crisp and light golden brown; do not burn or the garlic and oil will be unusable. Remove from the heat. Using a slotted utensil, immediately transfer the garlic chips to the prepared plate to drain. Reserve the garlic-cooking oil.

Add the chilies and 2 tablespoons of the reserved garlic-cooking oil (save the remainder for another use) to a large heavy skillet. Set over medium-high heat. Add the pistachios and sauté for 1 to 2 minutes. Add the "falafel" spice and salt and stir until the pistachios are coated with spice and heated through, 3 to 4 minutes. Remove from heat. Transfer the pistachios and chilies to a serving bowl. Add the garlic chips and toss well. Serve warm or at room temperature.

Beet Purée with Tahini and Date Syrup

Tomer Niv, the chef at Rama's Kitchen in Netaf, serves this purée as an appetizer with his freshly baked focaccia, brought to the table piping hot directly out of the taboon (clay oven). He garnishes it with spiced garbanzo beans and a few dashes of tahini sauce. If you want to make the date syrup yourself, have a look at blogger Tori Avey's website, www.ToriAvey.com.

2 pounds (1 kg) beets
1/2 cup (120 ml) silan (date syrup)
   or maple syrup
1/3 cup (80 ml) olive oil
Salt
1/2 cup (120 ml) tahini
3/4 cup (80 ml) water
1/2 lemon

Preheat the oven to 325°F (160°C). Wrap the beets in aluminum foil and bake until very tender, about 2 hours.

Let beets cool, then peel. Cut beets into pieces and place pieces in a blender or food processor. Add date or maple syrup and olive oil and purée. Season with salt. Transfer beet purée to a bowl.

Place the tahini in another bowl. Whisk in the water. Squeeze in juice from the lemon half. Season with salt. To serve, place a dollop of beet purée on plate. Top with tahini sauce.

Sardine Pizzas with Sage Oil, Cheddar Cheese, and Grapes

MAKES 4 PIZZAS

I spent a lot of time with Tomer Niv, the chef at Rama's Kitchen in Nataf, and admire his efforts to cook outside the box. This pizza is an excellent example of someone willing to try something different. If you cannot find fresh sardines, use small fresh mackerel, and if you cannot find fresh mackerel, find a way outside of your own box, but do not used canned fish. He actually uses under-ripe grapes, which are firm and sour and taste surprisingly good with the fresh fish and aromatic sage oil. Garnish with torn, fresh sage leaves.

3^1/$_4$ cups (415 g) 00 flour*, or 4 cups (500 g) all-purpose flour

1 cup (240 ml) plus 2 tablespoons water

1^1/$_2$ teaspoons salt

1 teaspoon active dry yeast

1 cup (240 ml) grape seed or vegetable oil (for frying)

3^1/$_2$ ounces (100 g) sage leaves

3 tablespoons olive oil

^{1}/$_2$ pound (230 g) aged cheddar cheese, finely grated

4 fresh sardines or small mackerels, skinned and filleted

12 firm green grapes, halved

Combine the flour, 1 cup (240 ml) water, salt, and yeast in the bowl of a stand mixer fitted with a bread hook. Mix on low speed until the dough is combined, starts to pull away from sides of the bowl, and forms a ball. (If dough appears too dry, add remaining water 1 tablespoon at a time.) Increase speed to medium and continue to mix until dough is smooth and elastic. Place dough in an oiled bowl. Cover and refrigerate at least 2 hours or overnight.

Divide dough into 4 balls. Roll each ball out on a floured work surface to 8 to 9-inch (20 to 23 cm) rounds that are about ^{1}/$_8$ inch (3 mm) thick. Set each round on a baking steel, pizza stone, or baking sheet.

Preheat the oven to 500°F (260°C), then lower to 450°F (230°C). Heat grape seed or vegetable oil to 325°F (160°C) in a medium-size heavy pot. Add sage leaves and fry until crispy (stand back; oil will splatter). Remove sage leaves using a slotted utensil and transfer to a blender or food processor. Add olive oil and purée. Brush sage-frying oil onto each pizza dough round. Divide the cheese among the rounds. Place two sardine fillets on each round. Arrange 6 grape halves cut-side down on each round. Bake until dough is cooked through and edges are crisp, cheese has melted, and fish is cooked, about 10 minutes. Serve pizzas immediately.

* "00" flour (Italian flour) is a very fine, powdery grind especially suited for making pizza dough and pasta. Several brands are available in the U.S.

Mushroom Kubeh Siniya

Siniya is both spelled and prepared differently throughout Israel. I asked my food journalist friend Ronit Vered to clarify this for me, and she told me that siniya is the name of the casserole dish used for both cooking and serving and that there are endless variations of what goes inside. This one is a vegetarian mushroom stew with a bulgur crust that Chef Jalil Jalil at Majda restaurant in Ein Rafa garnishes with three different tahini sauces—plain, burnt red pepper, and beet root—and a dollop of sweet and sour plum jam. Serve it with more tahini, fresh, soft pitas, and the Carrot, Cilantro, and Preserved Lemon Salad with Sweet Chili Dressing on page 87 and/or the Sweet and Sharp Beet Salad on page 88.

1 pound fine bulgur

1 scant cup (4 ounces; 120 g) all-purpose flour

$1/2$ cup (120 ml) vegetable oil

$1/2$ tablespoon smoked paprika or pimento

Salt and freshly ground pepper

Grated nutmeg

6 tablespoons olive oil

2 large onions, finely chopped

1 cup (240 ml) dry white wine

2 tablespoons Worcestershire sauce

2 pounds (approximately 1 kg) portobello mushrooms, trimmed, halved and sliced $1/4$ inch thick

Place the bulgur in a large bowl. Add enough boiling water to cover the bulgur by a scant 1 inch ($2^1/2$ cm). Let stand until bulgur absorbs all the water.

Transfer the bulgur to a stand mixer. Add the flour, vegetable oil, and paprika. Season with salt, pepper, and nutmeg to taste. Beat the mixture until it is soft, about 10 minutes, starting at a low speed and quickly working up to high speed. (Note that this might need to be done in two batches, depending on the size of the mixer.)

Heat the olive oil in a large heavy skillet over medium-high heat. Add the onions and cook until golden brown, stirring frequently, about 15 minutes. Season with salt and pepper. Stir in the wine and Worcestershire sauce and cook, stirring frequently, until all the liquid is absorbed, about 10 minutes. Add the mushrooms, season with salt and pepper, and cook until mushrooms are cooked through and have released and reabsorbed their juices, about 10 minutes; you want a dry mixture.

Preheat the oven to 475°F (245°C). Spread half of the bulgur mixture in the bottom of a 10 to 12-inch (25 to 30 cm) springform pan, deep cake pan, or baking dish. (If using a springform pan, set it on a baking sheet.) Top bulgur mixture with all of the mushroom mixture. Cover it with remaining bulgur mixture, spreading evenly and pressing down firmly. Bake until heated through, about 30 minutes. Serve immediately.

Eggplant Shish Barak

Shish barak, traditionally a meat-stuffed dumpling, is believed to have originated in pre-Islamic Persia and to have migrated over time throughout the Arab world. Chef Jalil Jalil at Majda restaurant serves his vegetarian version with a hot yogurt sauce flavored with garlic and turmeric. The shish baraks must be frozen overnight before they are cooked, so if you only want to make one or two servings, keep the rest frozen for those nights when you have nothing planned for dinner. As an alternative presentation, try pan-frying the boiled dumplings in olive oil until they are crispy on the outside and oozy on the inside.

FILLING

2 medium eggplants

1 cup ($^1/_2$ pound; 250 grams) labneh or Greek yogurt

3 tablespoons olive oil

1 large onion, minced

1 fresh hot chili, chopped

2 large garlic cloves, minced

$^1/_2$ cup (24 g) oregano leaves

Salt and freshly ground pepper

DOUGH

$3^3/_4$ cups (1 pound; 500 grams) all-purpose flour

$1^1/_2$ teaspoons salt

3 tablespoons olive oil

$1^1/_4$ cups (300 ml) water, room temperature

SERVE

Labneh, yogurt or sour cream

FOR FILLING: Preheat the oven to 400°F (200 C). Set eggplants on a baking sheet and bake until very soft, about 45 minutes. (Alternatively, grill or char eggplants over an open flame). Cool eggplants completely.

Place labneh in a large bowl. Heat the oil in a medium-size heavy skillet over medium heat. Add onion and sauté until softened, about 10 minutes. Add chili and garlic and sauté until fragrant, about 1 minute. Add the oregano and stir until fragrant but not brown, about 3 minutes. Add mixture to labneh and stir to blend.

Cut eggplants in half and scoop out the flesh. Transfer flesh to a cutting board and sprinkle with salt and pepper, then finely chop it and add to the bowl with labneh. Season generously with salt and pepper.

FOR DOUGH: Combine flour and salt in the bowl of stand mixer fitted with a bread hook. Beat in oil on low speed. Gradually beat in water on low speed. Increase speed to medium and continue mixing until dough is soft to the touch, about 5 minutes. (Alternatively, this can be done by hand.) Let stand 30 minutes.

Cut dough into 9 pieces. Roll each piece out on a lightly floured surface to $^1/_{12}$ inch (2 mm) thick, or as close as possible. Using a $2^1/_2$-inch (6 cm) drinking glass or cookie cutter, cut dough into rounds. Place 1 teaspoon filling onto each round, then fold into half-moon shapes, seal edges together, and pinch corners. Set on baking sheets and freeze overnight.

TO SERVE: Cook dumplings in small batches in a large pot of boiling water until soft, 3 to 5 minutes. Remove using a slotted utensil and serve on a plate or in a bowl, crowned with labneh, yogurt, or sour cream.

Chicken-Stuffed Artichoke Hearts with Olives, Chickpeas, and Saffron-Lemon Sauce

In the open kitchen at Chef Avi Levy's restaurant, Hamotzi, the enormous stockpots simmering on gas stoves evoke the way his grandmother cooked for him on kerosene burners in her small kitchen. I peered into one of the steaming cauldrons and saw artichoke hearts swimming next to plump chickpeas in a dark, rich sauce and wanted to jump in. Avi's hearty, rich recipes are prepared at night and served in copious portions to the jubilant crowds waiting to taste the soul food created by this master chef.

SAUCE

¹/₂ cup (120 ml) olive oil

1 onion, thinly sliced

5 garlic cloves, halved

2 teaspoons kosher salt

1 teaspoon freshly ground pepper

1 teaspoon curry powder

¹/₂ teaspoon ground cumin

4 to 5 saffron threads

Pinch of freshly grated nutmeg

2 cups (475 ml) chicken stock or broth

¹/₂ cup (120 ml) fresh lemon juice

1 cup (135 g) pitted green Moroccan or Sicilian olives

1 cup (150 g) cooked chickpeas, fresh or canned

ARTICHOKES

Vegetable or canola oil (for deep-frying)

6 tablespoons olive oil

2 medium onions, finely chopped

3 garlic cloves, minced

2 teaspoons freshly ground pepper

1 teaspoon kosher salt

1 teaspoon curry powder

(continued)

FOR SAUCE: Heat the olive oil in a large heavy pot over medium-high heat. Add the onion and sauté until golden, about 10 minutes. Add the garlic and the next 6 ingredients and stir well. Stir in the stock and lemon juice, then olives and chickpeas. Reduce heat to medium. Cover and simmer for 25 minutes.

FOR ARTICHOKES: Meanwhile, pour the vegetable oil into a large pot and heat to 375°F (190°C). Heat olive oil in a large heavy skillet over medium heat. Add the onion and sauté until golden, about 10 minutes. Add the garlic and next 5 ingredients and stir well. Place the chicken in large bowl. Transfer the onion mixture to bowl. Add the parsley and cilantro. Using clean hands, mix to incorporate all ingredients into chicken. Divide chicken mixture into 12 portions. Pat each portion into 1 artichoke heart. Whisk eggs in a bowl. Pour breadcrumbs into another bowl. Dip each artichoke heart into the egg, allowing excess to drip back into bowl. Dredge each artichoke heart in breadcrumbs, shaking off excess. Set on a baking sheet. Fry artichoke hearts in prepared oil until golden brown, 2 to 3 minutes per side. (Fry in batches if necessary; do not crowd.)

(continued)

1 teaspoon ground turmeric

1/2 teaspoon ground nutmeg

1 pound (450 g) ground chicken

1/2 cup (30 g) finely chopped
   parsley

1/2 cup (30 g) finely chopped
   cilantro

12 large fresh artichoke hearts

3 large eggs

1 1/2 cups (160 g) unseasoned
   breadcrumbs

TO FINISH: Transfer the fried stuffed artichoke hearts to the sauce. Reduce heat to medium. Cover and cook until artichoke hearts are soft, about 1 hour. Transfer two artichoke hearts to each plate. Pour sauce over. Serve immediately.

JARS OF PRESERVED LEMONS IN CHEF ARI LEVY'S KITCHEN IN HIS RESTAURANT HAMOTZI.

Falafel Shrimp with Eggplant Spread

Just one glance at the pink flesh of these stunning falafel and you might even forget that you once loved the classic chickpea version. Chef Jalil Jalil at Majda restaurant (an Arabic name that means strong, glorious woman) restaurant in Ein Rafa in the Judean Hills makes these from shrimp and a beet and horseradish mixture called hazart. JJ garnishes the falafel with an eggplant spread and a small dollop of hazart, which can also be mixed with yogurt and used as a dipping sauce for steamed artichokes.

EGGPLANT SPREAD

2 large eggplants

1 cup (245 g) labneh or Greek yogurt

Salt and freshly ground pepper

HAZART

2 medium beets, quartered

3.5 ounces (100 g) fresh horseradish root, peeled and chopped

FALAFEL SHRIMP

1 pound (450 g) peeled and deveined, raw shrimp, roughly chopped

3 cups (325 g) panko breadcrumbs

$1/2$ cup (120 g) prepared mayonnaise

Salt and freshly ground pepper

3 eggs

Vegetables oil (for deep-frying)

FOR EGGPLANT SPREAD: Preheat a grill to medium-low or preheat oven to 400°F (205°C). Grill the eggplants until soft, turning with tongs frequently, about $1^1/2$ hours, or roast in oven until soft, about 1 hour. Let cool. Peel charred skin off eggplants. Chop eggplant flesh and transfer to a bowl. Stir in labneh or yogurt. Season with salt and pepper. Cover and refrigerate until ready to use.

FOR HAZART: Place the beets and horseradish in a food processor. Pulse until finely chopped. Set aside.

FOR FALAFEL: Place the shrimp in large bowl. Stir in 1 cup (108 g) breadcrumbs, mayonnaise, and 2 tablespoons of beet mixture. (Reserve remaining beet mixture for another use.) Season shrimp generously with salt and pepper. Place remaining 2 cups (216 g) breadcrumbs in shallow bowl. Beat the eggs to blend in another shallow bowl. Using clean hands, form the shrimp mixture into $1^1/2$-inch (approximately 4 cm) balls; you should have about 24 balls. Dip each ball into egg, allowing excess to drip back into the bowl. Roll each ball in panko. Set on a baking sheet and repeat with remaining shrimp mixture, egg, and panko. Refrigerate for 2 hours.

Heat oil in a large heavy pot to 300°F (150°C). Fry shrimp balls (in batches, do not crowd) until golden brown, 3–4 minutes. Remove using a slotted utensil and drain on paper towels. Serve with the eggplant spread and remaining hazart.

Beet Purée with Tahini and Date Syrup

MAKES ABOUT 2 CUPS (475 ML)

Tomer Niv, the chef at Rama's Kitchen in Netaf, serves this purée as an appetizer with his freshly baked focaccia, brought to the table piping hot directly out of the taboon (clay oven). He garnishes it with spiced garbanzo beans and a few dashes of tahini sauce. If you want to make the date syrup yourself, have a look at blogger Tori Avey's website, www.ToriAvey.com.

2 pounds (1 kg) beets

$1/2$ cup (120 ml) silan (date syrup)
   or maple syrup

$1/3$ cup (80 ml) olive oil

Salt

$1/2$ cup (120 ml) tahini

$3/4$ cup (80 ml) water

$1/2$ lemon

Preheat the oven to 325°F (160°C). Wrap the beets in aluminum foil and bake until very tender, about 2 hours.

Let beets cool, then peel. Cut beets into pieces and place pieces in a blender or food processor. Add date or maple syrup and olive oil and purée. Season with salt. Transfer beet purée to a bowl.

Place the tahini in another bowl. Whisk in the water. Squeeze in juice from the lemon half. Season with salt. To serve, place a dollop of beet purée on plate. Top with tahini sauce.